BEADING WITH GEMSTONES

BEADING WITH GEMSTONES

Beautiful Jewelry, Simple Techniques

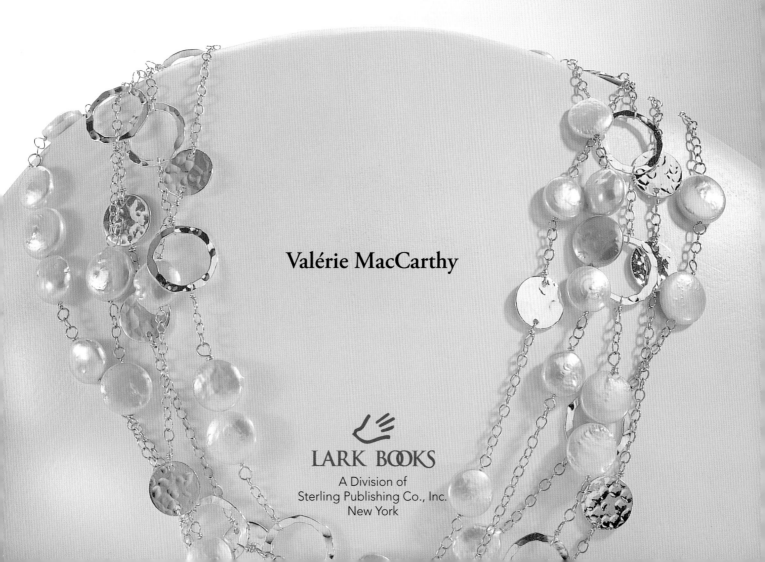

Valérie MacCarthy

LARK BOOKS
A Division of
Sterling Publishing Co., Inc.
New York

Senior Editor: **Valerie Van Arsdale Shrader**

Line Editor: **Vivian Rothe**

Art Director: **Kristi Pfeffer**

Cover Designer: **Cindy LaBreacht**

Associate Editor: **Nathalie Mornu**

Associate Art Director: **Shannon Yokeley**

Art Production Assistant: **Jeff Hamilton and Travis Medford**

Editorial Assistance: **Mark Bloom**

Editorial Intern: **Katrina Usher**

Art Intern: **Marshall Hudson**

Illustrators: **Bonnie Brooks and J'aime Allene**

Photographer: **Stewart O'Shields**

Library of Congress Cataloging-in-Publication Data

MacCarthy, Valérie, 1975-
  Beading with gemstones : beautiful jewelry, simple techniques / Valérie MacCarthy. -- 1st ed.
    p. cm.
  Includes index.
  ISBN-13: 978-1-57990-887-4 (hc-plc with jacket)
  ISBN-10: 1-57990-887-X
  1. Jewelry making. 2. Beadwork. I. Title.
  TT212.M25 2006
  739.27--dc22
                    2006100853

10 9 8 7 6 5 4 3 2 1

First Edition

Published by Lark Books, A Division of
Sterling Publishing Co., Inc.
387 Park Avenue South, New York, N.Y. 10016

Text © 2007, Valérie MacCarthy
Photography © 2007, Lark Books
Illustrations © 2007, Lark Books

Distributed in Canada by Sterling Publishing,
c/o Canadian Manda Group, 165 Dufferin Street
Toronto, Ontario, Canada M6K 3H6

Distributed in the United Kingdom by GMC Distribution Services,
Castle Place, 166 High Street, Lewes, East Sussex, England BN7 1XU

Distributed in Australia by Capricorn Link (Australia) Pty Ltd.,
P.O. Box 704, Windsor, NSW 2756 Australia

If you have questions or comments about this book, please contact:
Lark Books
67 Broadway
Asheville, NC 28801
(828) 253-0467

Manufactured in China

ISBN 13: 978-1-57990-887-4
ISBN 10: 1-57990-887-X

For information about custom editions, special sales, premium and corporate purchases, please contact Sterling Special Sales Department at 800-805-5489 or specialsales@sterlingpub.com.

CONTENTS

INTRODUCTION

I'm sure you've worn many different pieces of jewelry, from the simplest plastic band around your wrist to perhaps a very beautiful gold necklace handed down from generations. Many of your favorite pieces likely contain gemstones, such as amethyst, turquoise, or pearl. You've probably noticed that most contemporary jewelry containing these stones has a relaxed yet elegant look. Instead of having a perfectly shaped ring or necklace, many designers now tend toward organic composition of their pieces. Stones no longer need to be perfectly cut or polished. There's more playfulness and much more color in the pieces. In this book, I'll teach you how to create your own jewelry like this using a variety of gemstones.

The pieces you'll find here have an eclectic balance of styles: vintage and trendy, funky and sophisticated, East meets West. Some have a more classic design, such as the simple but elegant Harmony earrings (page 88) and the three-stranded City Nights necklace (page 114). Others break away from the norm to create the organic feel I love so much, like the clustered stones in the Starburst bracelet (page 101) and the flurry of pearls intermingled with sterling silver disks and hoops in the Snow necklace (page 81).

I started making jewelry as a child. Before being bitten by the fashion bug, I was already collecting stones, fascinated by their colors and beauty. One day, my grandmother gave me a box containing some seed beads and a bit of string. That was enough to hook me on the thrill of creating my own original designs, which were worn by all members of the family, including my grandfather! As I grew older, my career as a professional opera singer took up most of my time. While traveling from continent to continent working, I was introduced to beadwork from many cultures. As time passed, my need to work with my hands returned. Aside from all the seed beads still left over from my youth, I also started working with other materials, such as larger beads, crystals, feathers, ribbon, and even leather. Little by little, my fascination with natural stones resurfaced, and they are once again my passion.

There are hundreds of thousands of stones out there to choose from, so feel free to play around with the designs you find in this book. Mix and match the stones you love and have fun discovering your inner artist. If, for example, your favorite color is blue, why not try mixing lapis lazuli with chalcedony? Or why not use a few unexpected colors together, such as amber (yellow) with rose quartz (pink) and peridot (olive green)? When you get to the

projects section of the book, remember to let your muse guide you. Depending on your personal taste, you decide whether a design needs a little more or a little less. The important thing to remember is to have fun.

To help you learn about gemstones, I've dedicated part of the book to describing the stones—their colors, interesting facts about them, and even healing properties they are said to possess. The first chapter, *Learning About Gemstones*, and the appendix, *Identifying Gemstones*, will guide you into a better understanding of and appreciation for these wonderful (and often stunning) materials.

You'll also find a section to help you get started in jewelry making. This includes a guide to the tools you'll need and tips about your work space. Basic techniques are described and illustrated in the next chapter. I recommend you read through all of this section before getting started, as it will prepare you for any project you choose to create. Finally, the projects section provides complete instructions for making 30 different pieces of jewelry using gemstones. While the focal points of each piece are the gorgeous stones themselves, I also incorporate seed beads and glass beads, as well as chain and wire work in my creations.

Now you're ready to go! Let's begin by learning more about the gemstones.

Learning About Gemstones

Semiprecious stones are the primary focus of this book, and they have been the primary focus of my designs for a long time. Why? Because they're beautiful, and wearing them makes us feel beautiful. But that's not all. The attraction to gemstones has always been tied to their incredible colors and ability to play with light. Throughout the ages, gemstones have been objects to treasure and collect, important both as commodities and as symbols of wealth. To fully appreciate the materials with which you'll be working, let's spend just a few minutes discussing these special stones.

(Left to right)
Topaz, Coral, Lapis lazuli

What Is a Gemstone?

There's no exact definition to describe gems or gemstones—some have described them simply as "ornamental stones." But there are a number of specific characteristics that we ascribe to gemstones; color may be the most important to you, but some others include their atomic structure, hardness, gravity, and cleavage, or fracture. Since you'll be purchasing stones that will have already been cut and identified for you, you won't need to know much about the scientific techniques used to identify the raw material. But you're probably interested in some general information about the stones you'll use to make your jewelry.

Gemstones are most often minerals (such as topaz), but they can be organic (like coral) or, in rare cases, rock (such as lapis lazuli). All of these can be referred to as gemstones.

Agate

Clear quartz

Minerals

A mineral is an inorganic solid crystalline structure that's found in the Earth's crust. Depending on the mineral, its crystalline formation can be clearly evident, as in this clear quartz, or too small for the naked eye to see, like this agate. Sometimes minerals are referred to as crystals, which have been studied for centuries. In fact, the word crystal comes from the Greek word *krystallos*, or *kryos*, meaning "icy cold." It was once believed that rock crystal was ice that had frozen so hard it would never melt! This would almost seem to be true in the case of the most precious mineral of all, the diamond, which is rare and only exists in certain parts of the world. Other more common minerals, such as quartz, are abundant throughout the world. All crystals can be considered gemstones, but not all are suitable to be fashioned into jewelry.

Organic Stones

Organic gems are derived from living things, such as animals and plants, and they come in the form of amber, fossils, coral, and pearls. Although all of them are classified as organic gems, each has been formed in a unique manner. For instance, amber is pine-tree resin that fossilized 50 million years ago, coral is the secreted skeleton from the marine organisms called coral polyps, and fossils originate from shells and bones of animals that were trapped in layers of rock.

Fossil

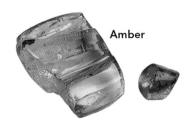

Amber

Pearls

Gemstones Qualities

Each type of gemstone has its own distinctive characteristics. As you become familiar with these qualities, you'll find that you can correctly identify most gemstones, and at the same time you'll be making good decisions about which stones to use for specific pieces.

Hardness

One way to identify a gemstone is by its specific hardness. All minerals can be placed on Mohs' scale of relative hardness, which was devised by German mineralogist Friedrich Mohs in 1812. As an aid in classifying the hardness of minerals, he selected 10 readily available minerals and placed them in order on the scale so that a specific mineral could scratch only the minerals listed above it, but none of those below it. Minerals of the same hardness can also scratch each other.

Pearls are formed naturally inside mollusks such as oysters to counteract the irritating effects of sand inside the shell. The mollusk covers the grain of sand with layers of nacre and, over time, the little grain of sand turns into a pearl. Cultured pearls, which are also considered gemstones, are formed when humans help along this natural process by placing the irritant in the jaws of the mollusk.

Rocks

A rock is a combination, or aggregate, of two or more minerals. We've all called a diamond a rock, but don't be fooled, because a diamond is no rock! Stones that are a combination of one or more minerals, such as lapis lazuli, labradorite, and moonstone, are designated as rocks.

Mohs' Hardness Scale

Following are Mohs' 10 minerals, with 1 (talc) being the softest mineral and 10 (diamond) being the hardest.

1	Talc	**6**	Orthoclase feldspar
2	Gypsum	**7**	Quartz
3	Calcite	**8**	Topaz
4	Fluorite	**9**	Corundum
5	Apatite	**10**	Diamond

Most semiprecious stones that you'll be using to make the jewelry pieces in this book are in the 5 to 7 range on the scale. Organic stones are much softer, in the range of 2 and 3. Be especially careful when working with these softer stones, which include pearls, coral, and amber, because they can become scratched or chipped more easily than the harder stones.

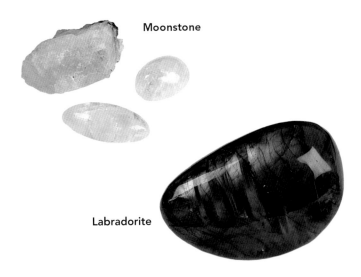

Moonstone

Labradorite

Tourmaline, with color variations

Crystalline varieties of quartz

Color

A crystal's color is often its most striking and attractive feature, and this is probably the quality that first attracted you to a particular stone. No doubt, color is an important consideration when you begin making your jewelry pieces.

Some minerals, known as allochromatic, occur in a variety of colors. Examples of these are quartz, diamond, toumaline, apatite, and fluorite. Other minerals referred to as idiochromatic always occur as the same color. For example, peridot is an idiochromatic mineral, always appearing green.

Peridot

Some stones may resemble each other to the naked eye (for instance, yellow topaz and citrine are commonly confused), but due to their specific chemical properties and ordered atomic structure, a gemologist can discern the difference. The opposite also holds true. For example, there are many different quartz varieties that look nothing like pure clear quartz. They've even been given completely different names, such as chalcedony, agate, and chrysoprase, but in fact these all belong to the same quartz family as clear quartz, amethyst, and citrine. It's important to be aware of these aspects of gemstone colors when selecting stones for your jewelry projects.

Chrysoprase

Chalcedony

Light

The play of light and its effect on color is one of the intriguing factors concerning gemstones, and you'll probably want to design your pieces with this characteristic in mind. The particular color of a stone is primarily due to dispersion, the breaking up of white light into a spectrum (rainbow). When light passes through a gemstone, some spectral colors are absorbed while others are reflected back. Those that are reflected back give the gem its color. With colorless stones, you may see flashes of color, often referred to as fire, which is also due to this dispersion of light.

The appearance of certain colors can be due to impurities in the stone, ironically enough. For example, amethyst is rock quartz containing trace amounts of ferric iron, and the rose colors in rose quartz are created by traces of manganese or titanium.

Rose quartz

Some crystals can make you think you're seeing double! This effect is called refraction, which occurs when light passing through a crystal is split into two rays. Because gems have more density than air, light slows down and bends, causing the double image.

Certain stones, such as moonstone and labradorite, play with light to cause effects that look similar to a soap bubble or an oil slick. This effect, which is caused by light reflecting off structures within the stone, is called interference, or sometimes opalescence or schiller.

Enhanced and Altered Stones

The appearance of some gemstones can be altered by heat, irradiation, staining, and oiling, and this may influence how you feel about using a certain stone in your jewelry pieces.

Amethyst

Citrine

Heat treatment is used either to enhance or to change a gem's color. In the case of amethyst, heating it will turn it to citrine. Irradiation also causes a stone to change color, and this can happen naturally from radioactive elements within the Earth's crust, or artificially, through human methods.

Staining can be done using stains, dyes, or chemicals. Some techniques coat the surface, while others change the entire stone. Staining can only be done on porous stones, which allow the color to enter into them. This technique is used to enhance a stone's color or to imitate another stone. For example, howlite, which is naturally white, is often dyed to imitate turquoise.

Oiling is used to enhance a stone by hiding the cracks and fissures. Emeralds and opals are often oiled to fill in their blemishes.

Know Your Gemstones

Creating gemstone jewelry is exciting and inspiring. The gemstones have a beauty of their own, even before being combined with other stones and precious metals to make rings, earrings, bracelets, and necklaces. Before you begin shopping for stones, I recommend that you get to know a little about them, especially the range of colors, characteristics, and identifying factors that make them unique. For a brief introduction to the many gemstones available for your jewelry, see the appendix on page 123.

Birthstones

Certain stones have traditionally been associated with months of the year. This came about after the breastplate of a high priest was discovered in Egypt containing these 12 stones. According to tradition, Hebrews took the 12 stones and assigned each one to represent their 12 tribes of Israel. But it was in the 18th century in Poland that wearing birthstones came into fashion. It was believed that the cosmic energy transmitted by the stones would resonate back to the wearer, creating positive energy that, in turn, would bring good luck and happiness.

Following is a list of traditional birthstones:

January: garnet, rose quartz

February: amethyst, onyx

March: aquamarine, tourmaline

April: diamond, zircon, crystal quartz

May: emerald, chrysoprase

June: pearl, moonstone

July: ruby, carnelian

August: peridot, onyx

September: sapphire, chrysolite

October: opal, pink tourmaline

November: topaz, citrine, smoky quartz

December: turquoise, zircon

Healing Stones

Throughout the ages, many cultures around the world have used stones for healing. Each type of stone has its own unique composition and emits a different vibration, making them of value in healing specific ailments.

Some stones are considered to have qualities for dissolving stress, others for unblocking chakras, and others for supporting the immune system and neutralizing negative energy. Traditional Chinese medicine has been using stones for healing for more than 5,000 years. Even without knowing the properties of the stones they're wearing, some have said they instinctively feel better when wearing them. A friend of mine swears that the rose quartz necklace I made for her helped her get pregnant!

Getting Started

Making your own gemstone jewelry is exciting and rewarding. You'll be thrilled as you see the project you have selected coming together, one step at a time. But first, especially if you're new to jewelry making, read through this section to find out about the stones and other jewelry materials, plus the tools and supplies that you'll need to create your project.

Before You Begin

Check the finished size of the piece you plan to make. If you want to make it smaller (shorter) or larger (longer), make changes as needed for all items in the materials list and mark changes as needed in the instructions.

Make sure you have all necessary materials, tools, and supplies. These include:

- Gemstone and accent beads
- Findings, such as clasps, head pins, jump rings, earring components
- Chain
- Wire
- Tools
- Supplies

Prepare your work space.

- Set aside all other projects in progress.
- Clean your work space.
- Organize the materials for your new project.

Practice new techniques using inexpensive materials.

Gemstone and Accent Beads

To make the gemstone jewelry designs in this book, you'll need a variety of fine gemstone beads. All of the designs use gemstones that have holes drilled into them, so they are technically called beads. I also use less-precious seed beads for accents. The process of selecting and shopping for just the right ones is one of the most exciting aspects of making your own jewelry.

I've used many different stones for these designs, but feel free to mix and match other stones in place of the ones you see. The best way to find your inner artist is by taking a risk and trying something new, even if it's only using another color or a different type of stone.

Some of the gemstones I've used are fairly common; others are rare. As you can imagine, the rarer the stone, the more valuable it is, and the more costly it is. Before you begin any project, check on the price and availability of the stones you plan to use.

Keep in mind that you can substitute many of the stones shown in the projects. For instance, where I may have used tourmaline, which is a pricey stone, you can substitute quartz or chalcedony, which are much more common and cost a fraction of the price of tourmaline. You'll have a beautiful piece of jewelry with either selection.

Do you already have a collection of gemstones and beads? Before shopping for new ones, take a fresh look at what you have on hand. You may discover that some of the projects in this book are perfect for stones you've stashed away, just waiting for you to find the perfect designs to show off their qualities.

After you've checked your own collection, visit several bead stores in your area to explore their resources and shop their inventory. What better way to become familiar with all that's involved in making gemstone jewelry? You'll be able to see firsthand the myriad beads and stones and learn more about their colors, shapes, and qualities. Many bead shops also offer how-to classes and workshops, an excellent means of discovering and learning new techniques. Be sure to check out coming shows and exhibits that you may want to attend. We all benefit from inspiration, and we all like to show off our latest work, especially to others who love to work with gemstones!

The Internet has become a valuable source for locating and purchasing beautiful stones and supplies directly from the manufacturers at affordable prices. Make use of online search resources and auction sites to find exactly the stones and supplies you're looking for.

Bead Sizes

All of the designs in this book require specified sizes of stones. Stones and beads are sized according to metric units of measure, with a stone's size usually determined by its diameter. If you're not familiar with metric measurements, you'll soon get to know the measurements that are most commonly used in making jewelry.

A slide caliper is a handy tool for measuring stones and beads, allowing you to measure their exact size. You'll want to have a caliper with you when you go shopping for stones so you can buy exactly the right size. See the guide to standard stone and bead sizes on page 122.

Bead Shapes

Stones come in all sorts of different shapes and sizes. You'll want to become familiar with the most common shapes. A visit to a bead shop or online research will provide answers to many of your specific questions about which stones are available in which specific shapes. I've included most of these shapes in the jewelry designs in this book.

Bicone: Diamond-shaped

Briolette: Teardrop-shaped bead with faceted sides or round with no flat sides

Disk or Coin: Round, flattened shape

Drop or Teardrop: Round with a soft point, pendant-shaped; the hole can be either horizontally through the top or vertically through the center

Nugget: Irregular

Oval: Egg-shaped, elliptical

Rondelle: Doughnut-shaped

Round: Ball-shaped

All of these different shapes can be faceted, smooth, or even rough. A faceted stone has flat surfaces cut into the stone. A diamond, for example, is almost always faceted. These facets throw off light, giving stones a sparkling effect. A smooth stone has no facets and is smooth to the touch. It is usually curved to give it a shape, and it has no sharp edges. A rough stone will often be in its unpolished state, but it can also be shaped this way to give it a more organic, natural look.

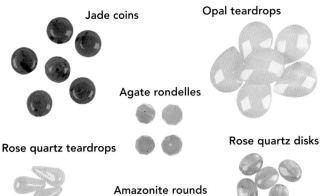

Jade coins

Opal teardrops

Agate rondelles

Rose quartz teardrops

Rose quartz disks

Amazonite rounds

Turquoise nuggets

Carnelian rounds

Amethyst teardrops

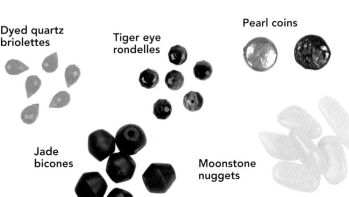

Dyed quartz briolettes

Tiger eye rondelles

Pearl coins

Jade bicones

Moonstone nuggets

Precious Metals

All the jewelry pieces in this book are made with either sterling silver or gold-filled precious-metal components.

Sterling silver is 92.5 percent pure silver. The remaining 7.5 percent is usually copper. Pure silver (99.9 percent) is not commonly used for jewelry because it is considered to be too soft.

Gold-filled is the name given to gold that has been mechanically bonded with heat and pressure to a less expensive metal, such as brass. This creates a fine metal, excellent for jewelry, without the expense of 14- or 24-karat gold. The amount of gold on gold-filled metals is 50 to 100,000 times thicker than the amount of gold used in making gold-plated metals. This is an important difference, one that you need to be aware of when purchasing precious metals for making jewelry, so don't be fooled into buying the wrong thing.

Seed Beads

Seed beads are wonderful to have on hand to use for details in your designs. While being just a tiny little thing, you'll be surprised how one small bead or several of them together can add depth to a piece of jewelry. I use them in several of the designs in this book, including the Spotlight (page 77) and Duet (page 62) necklaces.

Seed beads come in a dizzying array of sizes and colors, but they are grouped into categories according to shape.

The most common shape of seed bead is rocaille. It's an oval-shaped seed bead ranging in sizes from 1.15 mm to 9 mm. Depending on the manufacturer, some are uniform in size while others may vary. I always look for uniformity, and I prefer the smaller sizes to keep things clean and neat. Pay close attention to the center hole when choosing the beads, because some can be too small to slide onto wire. Oddly enough, large seed beads don't always have large holes.

Delica is another type of seed bead that I use extensively in my jewelry. These beads are known for their uniformity. They are user-friendly because of their extra-large hole, and they are available in only one size (2.1 mm). While similar to rocaille beads, delicas have flat sides instead of curved ones, so you can create a flat, straight line when stringing them together.

Bugle beads are also popular. They are tubular, similar to delicas, but longer. They come in lengths from 4 mm to more than 20 mm.

Other shapes of seed beads are square, hex or hexagonal, and triangular.

Wire

Wire is a beader's best friend, acting in somewhat the same manner as glue to join gemstones, beads, and findings. At the same time, wire is an integral part of jewelry design, contributing both form and function. Wire can be described in four major categories: size, hardness, color (or metal), and shape.

Wire size is often described by its gauge, a form of measurement used in the United States that indicates the diameter of wire. The higher the gauge number, the thinner the wire. See the chart on page 122.

In this book, I've used three gauges of wire: 26, 24, and 22. The 22-gauge wire is used primarily to make earring loops. The 26- and 24-gauge wires are slightly thinner, and they are most often used in making bracelets and necklaces. The size of holes in the stones selected for the piece often determines the gauge of wire. Small holes require thin wire, but thicker wire is sometimes better because it is stronger. As a rule, thinner wire is better with small stones because it is less cumbersome, and thicker wire is better with large stones because it provides better support.

Depending on the type of chain you're using for a particular piece, you can blend in the loops of wire by closely matching the wire gauge to the diameter of the links in the chain, as with the Countless bracelet (page 46).

Wire hardness has three categories: half-hard, soft, and dead-soft. Half-hard is the only hardness of wire used for the designs in this book.

Wire is defined by its color, or metal, with choices including silver, gold, and copper, as well as a variety of nonmetallic colors. I've selected designs for this book using the more precious metals of sterling silver and gold-filled. You can substitute alloys, which are a blend of less expensive metals. However, I find that there is a special thrill in working with precious metals, especially when these high-quality materials are combined with gemstones. With sterling silver and gold-filled wires, your jewelry pieces will be more valuable and long-lasting.

Wire comes in many shapes. For this collection, all of the pieces are made with simple round wire. As you gain experience in making and designing jewelry, you may want to work with other wire shapes, such as square, half-round, triangular, and twisted wires.

I recommend that you always have inexpensive wire on hand to practice new designs and test new techniques. Switch to the more expensive sterling silver or gold-filled wire when you've decided exactly how you want to make your piece, after you're certain that you've mastered the necessary techniques.

Findings

Findings are prefabricated jewelry components such as clasps, earring backs, jump rings, head pins, and small metal beads used to complete your jewelry. They come in many metals, shapes, and sizes. If you prefer, you can make some of these from wire (see Basic Techniques, beginning on page 20). All of the findings used in this book are either sterling silver or gold-filled. Always be sure to select the same type of metal as the wire and chain in the piece you'll be making.

I recommend that you keep on hand a supply of sterling silver and gold-filled beads in a variety of sizes. These are ideal for adding detail and depth to many designs. The 2-mm and 3-mm sizes are the only ones you'll need for the designs in this book, but you may want to experiment with others.

Metal bead

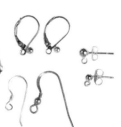

Earring backs

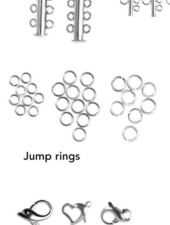

Slide clasps

Head pins

Jump rings

Clasps

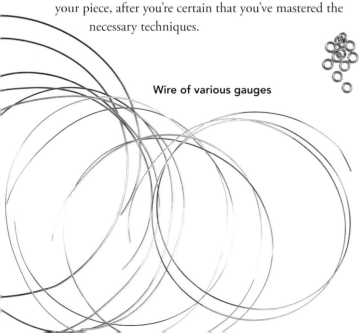

Wire of various gauges

Chain of various sizes

Tools and Supplies

You'll need only a few basic tools, plus supplies that you may already have on hand, to begin making the jewelry projects that you'll find in this book. Try making a few simple pieces, and then gradually add new tools to your collection as you gain experience.

Three Basic Tools

To make gemstone and wire jewelry that is both pleasing to wear and professional in workmanship, you'll need three basic jewelry-making tools: chain-nose pliers, round-nose pliers, and wire cutters. These tools, designed especially for working with the relatively lightweight wires and chains, are smaller and lighter than similar standard-size pliers and wire cutters found at your local hardware store. Bigger is not better in this case. The thinner and smaller the tools, the easier it will be for you to make the designs in this book; bigger just gets bulky.

Chain-nose pliers act almost like tiny little fingers for me, grabbing on and holding tight to the wire. These pliers are also excellent for opening and closing jump rings, bending wire, and accessing tight areas where your fingers would never be able to reach.

Round-nose pliers are primarily used to make loops (see Making Twisted Wire Loop Links, page 20) and for twirling wire and head pins (see Working with Head Pins, page 23). Because these pliers are tapered, you can vary the size of the loop you want to make depending on where along the jaws of the pliers you place the wire.

Chain

This book focuses on gemstone jewelry using chain as a part of the design. Purchase commercial chain at bead stores or online, where you'll find it sold from large spools in sizes ranging from large and thick to thin and delicate. For most of these gemstone designs, I've used thin chain with gauges between 1 mm and 2 mm. This small-gauge chain allows the focus of the jewelry piece to be on the stone instead of the chain.

I use large-gauge chain, such as 2.5 mm and 3.5 mm, for toggles on necklaces so that the clasps can easily fit into the links. I also use these larger-link chain for certain designs, so having a variety on hand is always useful.

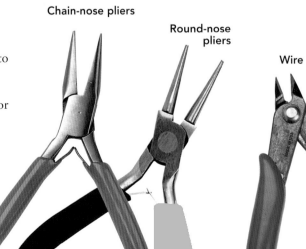

Chain-nose pliers

Round-nose pliers

Wire cutters

If you want to make the same size loop every time, use a permanent marker to mark the spot on the jaw where you place the wire. By always placing your wire at that same spot, you can consistently make loops that are identical in size.

If you're just starting out in making jewelry, you'll find that inexpensive chain-nose and round-nose pliers work nicely for you. As you expand your range of projects and techniques, you may want to add to your tool collection and purchase higher quality tools that provide additional precision.

Wire cutters are used for cutting all wire and chain. Because you'll sometimes be working in very small spaces, you'll definitely want a thin pair of wire cutters. The narrower the wire cutters, the easier it will be to get into those tight spots. I recommend that you also have a larger, sturdier pair of wire cutters for regular use when you're not cutting in those tight spaces. This will allow you to extend the life of your thin pair. Wire cutters eventually wear out and the tips can break or become dull with use, so you'll have to replace them occasionally.

Handy Tools and Supplies

Large rubberized round-nose pliers are excellent for making earring loops (page 24). These are not readily available commercially, but you can make them yourself with just two items from your local hardware store. Purchase a pair of standard round-nose pliers and plastic (or rubber) dip. The dip, which is available in a variety of colors, is a liquid form of plastic that feels like rubber after it dries. Use the dip to coat the jaws of these larger pliers, being careful not to coat the hinges. You may need to dip the jaw tips several times to get them thickly coated. Hang the pliers to make sure the coating dries evenly. The dip will dry quickly, and you'll have another handy tool!

Nylon-jaw pliers are the tool to use for flattening wire projects, such as the Kokopelli earrings (page 91). The rubberized round-nose pliers also work for this, but the jaws of the nylon-jaw pliers are flat and hard, getting the job done more efficiently without damaging your work.

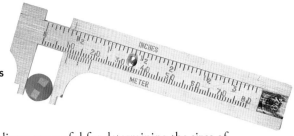
Slide calipers

Slide calipers are useful for determining the sizes of stones, beads, and chains. Place the stone or component you want to size between the two jaws of the caliper and slide them tight. The size will be indicated on top of the caliper. This little tool comes in handy when shopping for stones. As I said earlier, take slide calipers with you when you're shopping, and measure the stones at the store so you get the proper size for your jewelry project.

Include scissors, a ruler, adhesive tape, and a permanent marker in your tool kit. I frequently use tape for hanging my projects while I work on them (often on my lamp). It's much easier to see what you're doing when a piece is hanging rather than lying flat on a work surface.

Make sure the ruler has both U.S. and metric measurements. You'll find that you're often measuring lengths of chain and wire while you're making a piece, and you'll be measuring your work in progress, too.

A needle threader comes in handy when you're using thread or elastic cord with stones that have very small holes. When working with these, I often put a needle threader through the hole of the bead, place a tip of the string through the wires of the needle threader, and pull the threader back through with the string. Keep several of these needle threaders on hand, because they are fragile and can break easily.

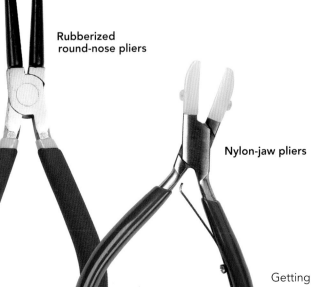

Rubberized round-nose pliers

Nylon-jaw pliers

Glue

Glue is useful for making certain that all materials are completely secure. Bead stores carry a variety of glues and cements. The best cement for gemstone jewelry dries clear and is made specifically for use with stones and metal. You can sometimes use cyanoacrylate, or permanent, glue. Its fast-drying quality is useful but also dangerous; if you aren't extremely careful, you may find a stone firmly adhered to your finger.

You may want to use a few tiny drops of glue after your project is completed. At that point, you can place a tiny drop on the holes of strung beads to cement them into place. Also, filling a bead hole with glue will sometimes make the hole less visible. Keep in mind that the glue must have a pinpoint precision nozzle for this kind of delicate work.

Special Tools

Working with a jig is a lot of fun, and I've included several pieces in this book that begin with a wire shape created on a jig, including the Olé! earrings (page 111) and the Starburst bracelet (page 101). I made the wire shapes for the Olé! earrings with a curved-grid jig, but you can make the same piece using a straight-grid jig or even round-nose pliers.

When making rings, you'll appreciate using a ring mandrel, which is marked with standard ring sizes. The mandrel also serves as a sturdy tool on which to build your ring. I used a mandrel in making the Sea Bundle ring (page 108).

Straight-grid jig

Ring mandrel

Cleaning cloth

Polishing and Cleaning Supplies

Jewelry can tarnish over time, especially sterling silver jewelry, so you'll want to have some jewelry cleaner on hand. There are a variety of cleaning supplies to choose from, varying from cleaning cloths to liquid to dip your jewelry into. Whatever you choose, make sure it's safe for the jewelry you want to clean.

Sterling silver cleaner is very strong and can damage soft or porous stones such as pearls. For more delicate pieces such as these, I recommend using a cleaner especially made for delicate stones. Check with a local jewelry store for these special cleaners, or shop for them online.

Organizing Your Work Space

Create your work space with care and consideration. Make it a place of your own, where you can relax, focus, and work without interruption.

Setting Up Your Work Space

Spending a few minutes preparing your area before you begin will make your work time on a new piece of jewelry much more productive and fun.

Following are a few items to include in your work space:

A very bright light, preferably a desk light, placed so that it shines right on your work space, is of utmost importance. The best ones re-create natural lighting, which is bright but won't tire your eyes.

A felt or velvet pad to work on helps keep small beads and stones from rolling away. Bead shops often carry pads made especially for this purpose, but a piece of felt or velvet also works nicely.

A set of five to 10 little bowls or trays approximately 2 inches (5.1 cm) in diameter will hold the stones and beads you're working with, helping to keep things organized. Use one of these as a miniature garbage can for leftover pieces of wire and bits of chain that accumulate as you work.

A necklace display comes in handy so you can get a good idea of how the necklace will fall naturally. You can also work on your piece while it's hanging on the display.

Storing Stones and Supplies

The storage of your stones and supplies is also important. The more organized you are, the easier and faster it will be to find what you're looking for. Here are storage tips that I've found to be lifesavers:

Use small storage cases used for nails and screws from the hardware store to store stones and beads. These cases are perfectly sized for holding and organizing your goodies. They come in a variety of sizes, giving you the option of picking what's right for you and the size of stones you want to store.

Clear plastic cases or boxes are handy for larger items, such as your tools and supplies. You can see into them without having to open each one to find out what's in the case. Shoe boxes also make good storage boxes. Be sure to put a label on the outside so you don't have to open each one to find what you're looking for.

Little plastic storage bags from the bead store are a great way to keep findings separate and sealed so that a bump or spill won't cause chaos in your supplies. Use a permanent marker to

label each one (clasps, jump rings, head pins, earring backs, silver and gold beads, and more).

If you have many different kinds of findings and find it difficult to keep track of all those baggies, organize them in accordion file cases. Small cases designed specifically for storing beads and findings are also widely available.

Creating Your Own Logo

In some of my pieces you might notice that I added a little personal touch. I created my own logo out of twisted wire and placed it on pieces such as the Rainbow earrings (page 39).

This is a great way to show that a piece is made by you. Believe it or not, it immediately adds a bit of value. The people you will be making jewelry for will love showing off this little tag, proud that they own a special piece made by you! So play around a little with your wire and come up with something you feel represents you. Then simply add it to your necklaces, bracelets, or earrings as you desire.

Bead storage

Basic Techniques

The gemstone jewelry projects in this book require mastery of a few basic techniques. Once you are adept in these simple methods, you'll be able to tackle any design you choose.

Using the Basic Tools

I always have the three tools that I discussed on page 16 right at my fingertips when making jewelry: chain-nose pliers, round-nose pliers, and wire cutters. You may already have similar tools in a toolbox for household use, but don't be fooled, because these are too large for making the projects in this book. Jewelry-making pliers and wire cutters are smaller than the ones from the hardware store, and you'll need to buy them at a craft or bead store or online. As you find yourself with both hands working closely together in those tight spots to attach, bend, wrap, loop, and snip, you'll be glad you have the smaller sizes!

As a rule, hold the tools as you would a bicycle handle. The same squeezing action you make with the hand brakes to slow down or stop a bicycle is all you need to hold, bend, or cut a jewelry wire or chain.

Working with Wire

I've found there are two different methods when it comes to working with wire. You may want to try both of them, and then continue to use the one that you prefer.

The first method is to cut a length of wire as specified in the materials list of the project that you're going to be making. As you work through each step to make the project, you'll be working from one end of the wire, making loops and links as needed, and then snipping them off. As you continue to use this same piece of wire throughout the project, it will get shorter each time you snip off a loop or link. When you've completed the project, you'll have used the entire length of wire.

The other method, which is how I usually do it, is to work directly off the spool. Wire is almost always purchased on spools, and I never remove the wire or cut it from the spool until I have to. Instead, I work directly from the spool, making new loops or links as needed, and then cutting them off. I find that this makes less waste, because I don't end up with odd lengths of wire that are too short. However, if you decide to use this method, it's important to be certain before beginning a project that you have enough wire on your spool to complete it.

Making Twisted Wire Loop Links

This type of link is my favorite way of attaching any component to any other component, whether it's a bead to a chain, a bead to another bead, or a chain to a clasp. You'll be using it frequently when making the gemstone designs in this book. Practice with inexpensive wire until you've mastered it, then cut the beads loose. I've found this linking technique to be more secure and durable than using a jump ring because it involves twisting and locking the wire into place.

1. To make a twisted wire loop link, use round-nose pliers to grip a piece of wire ¾ inch (1.9 cm) from the end. Bend the wire around the tip of the pliers to form a loop (photo 1).
2. Remove the pliers and grip the loop itself with chain-nose pliers. Twist the two wire ends around each other one and one-half times to secure. Make sure the longer wire is facing straight up from the loop. Now use wire cutters to cut off the shorter wire end close to the twist (photo 2). You've now made the first half of the loop link. Select the stone or bead that you are using for the design and slide it onto the wire.
3. To make the second part of the loop link, bend the wire at a 45° angle and repeat the process of looping on this end of the wire (photo 3). Wrap the wire end around to secure it, and then cut off the wire close to

photo 1

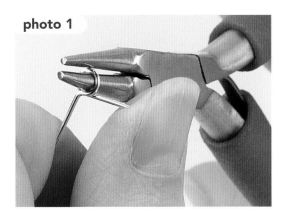

photo 2

photo 3

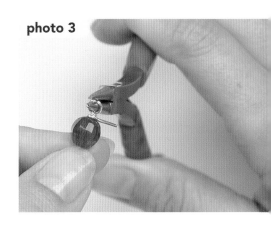

photo 4

Loop link
without bead

Forward
facing link

Side
facing link

the twist (photo 4). For some of my jewelry designs, I use this link without a stone. To make this type of link, follow the technique described on page 20 but don't place a stone on the wire after you've completed the first loop. Make the second loop, and then wrap the wire end around the twist you just completed to secure the piece.

If you need to join links, you can build the next one by attaching it to the link you've just created. If you're attaching the link to a chain, be sure to place the chain link on the loop before closing it.

You'll be using a similar technique to attach briolette-shaped stones, as well as pearls and stones with holes drilled at the top instead of through the center. To attach these stones, slide the wire through the hole, allowing ¾ inch (1.9 cm) to pass through to the other side. Bend both wire ends up until they cross tightly. Twist the wires around to secure and cut off the shorter wire end. Bend the remaining wire at a 45° angle, and use round-nose pliers to make a loop. Hold the loop with chain-nose pliers and wrap the wire around the twist you just completed to secure the piece.

When attaching these stones, make sure the direction of the loop brings attention to the stone instead of the wire. If you've already completed your loop and it is not facing the direction you prefer, simply grip the loop with round-nose pliers and give it a small, additional twist to make the loop either forward-facing or side-facing, whichever is needed for your piece. Following up with this small but important detail will allow the stone to be the focus of your design.

You'll notice that I often say to bend the wire 45°. Bending the wire in this manner keeps the loop centered above the bead (photo 5). If you don't bend the wire, you'll find your loop will tend to veer to one side. This simple 45° bend will prevent this from happening.

photo 5

Making Basic Loop Links

Now that you've learned how to make a twisted wire loop link, a basic loop link will seem like child's play. Although I don't often use this link, I needed it for the Harmony earrings (page 88).

photo 6

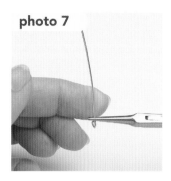
photo 7

1. To make this link, hold the very tip of the wire with round-nose pliers, and then rotate the tool until the wire tip is touching the side of the wire (photo 6).
2. Keep the pliers placed through the hole, but rotate them so the outer jaw is now against the straight wire. Bend the straight wire 45° to center the loop (photo 7).

Using Jump Rings

Jump rings are sometimes used to join beads and other components when making jewelry. A jump ring requires a simple technique to open and close the ring. Use two pliers, holding one in each hand, to carefully open the ring. Move one end of the ring toward you and the other end away from you, as shown (photo 8). Never pull apart the ends of a jump ring, because that will weaken the metal. To close a jump ring, reverse this procedure to gently bring the two ends back together.

photo 8

Making Catches and Clasps

Many of the projects in this book have a catch on one end and a clasp on the other end. A simple catch is a variation of the twisted wire loop link (page 20). To make this type of catch, use round-nose pliers to grip the wire ¾ inch (1.9 cm) from the end. Loop the wire around the pliers. Slide this loop onto one end of the necklace, whether a chain or a beaded loop link. Grip this loop with chain-nose pliers and twist the wires around to secure. Cut off the shorter wire end close to the twist.

Using large rubberized round-nose pliers, loop the remaining wire to form a large loop. If you don't have rubberized pliers, use your small round-nose pliers, wrapping the wire around the fattest part of the jaws to form this large loop.

After forming this large loop, hold it with the chain-nose pliers and wrap the wire around the twist you just completed. Cut off the excess wire close to the twist.

Wire catch

Another type of catch you may want to consider is a toggle, which is simply a piece of chain with links large enough for the clasp to go through. The toggle chain, added at the back of the necklace, can either replace the catch or be in addition to it, whichever you choose.

Toggles are handy when you are making necklaces for others and are not sure of the neck size. With a toggle, the length of the necklace can be adjusted as needed, and it provides interesting detail on the back of the necklace.

To make a toggle, simply make a twisted wire loop link with or without a bead (page 20) and attach about 2 inches (5.1 cm) of large-link chain to it. Place a few beads on a head pin and attach it to the other end of the chain to complete the toggle.

I almost always use prefabricated clasps, but you can make them, if you prefer. To learn more about this technique, see the instructions for the Spotlight necklace (page 77).

Working with Head Pins

Head pins are wonderful little findings that allow you to dangle beads from chains and looped wire. Three common types are ball-end, flat-end, and eye pins, all of which can be purchased ready-made. I usually prefer ball-end, because I find them to be more attractive, adding yet one more detail to the design. I chose to use flat-end head pins in the Ivy (page 99) and Fantastical earrings (page 65) because these seem to disappear completely, a nice effect when the design needs no additional detail. You can easily make your own decorative eye pins, as well as add elegant detail to purchased head pins; both methods are shown as follows.

Eye Pins

photo 9   **photo 10**

1. An eye pin is simply a piece of wire with a basic loop link at the end. I prefer to make these a little more fancy, such as for the Chandelier earrings (page 104). To make a decorative eye pin, grip the tip of a piece of wire (such as 24-gauge) with the very tip of your round-nose pliers (photo 9).
2. Wrap the wire around the top jaw of the pliers one or two times (photo 10), depending on the look you prefer. Keeping the pliers in place, bend the wire 45° to center the loop. Then continue to work with them as you would a standard pin.

Twirled Head Pins

I like the effect of twirling purchased head pins and covering them with seed beads. They add a certain daintiness when mixed in among stones and beads, as shown in the Lily earrings (page 56).

1. To make a twirled head pin, grip the end of the pin with round-nose pliers. Wrap the pin around one jaw of the round-nose pliers by gripping the end of the

photo 11

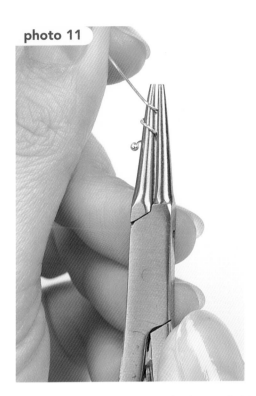

Twirled head pin

pin and twirling it around (photo 11). To continue the twist, release the pliers, rotate the pin slightly, grip again with the pliers, and twist. Because the jaw of the pliers is tapered, be careful not to taper your twist.

2. To keep it even, flip the head pin when it is halfway twisted and continue wrapping it around the jaw. Leave a straight length of ¾ inch (1.9 cm) at the end. Select seed beads and slide them onto the twirled head pin, stopping when you reach the straight part of the pin, which you'll use to attach the pin to the piece of jewelry.

For most jewelry projects, you'll cover the head pin with seed beads or stones so that it doesn't show. However, another nice way to use head pins is to display them a bit, as in the Fireworks necklace (page 30). To do so, simply place one to three beads on the head pin, leaving most of the head pin empty. Now, instead of bending the head pin immediately above the beads, bend it much higher up. Grip the pin with round-nose pliers and loop it around. Then attach the pin to your chain and loop the wire around to secure. Attaching the head pins this way allows the beads to move around, adding interest to the design.

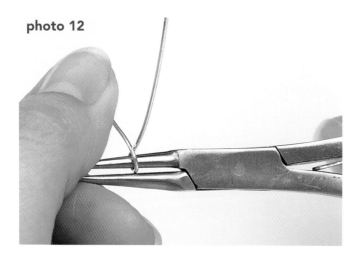

photo 12

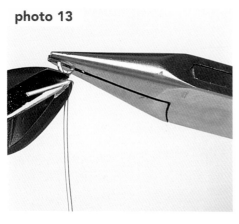

photo 13

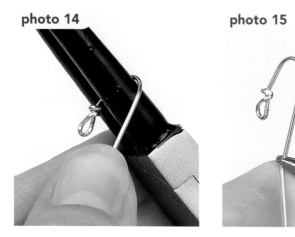

photo 14

photo 15

photo 16

Making Earring Loops

I like to make my own ear wires, which I'll call earring loops.

1. To make an earring loop, use wire cutters to cut a 2½-inch (6.4 cm) length of 22-gauge wire. Use round-nose pliers to grip the wire ¾ inch (1.9 cm) from the end. Wrap the wire around the pliers to form a circle (photo 12).
2. Grip the loop with the chain-nose pliers and twist the two wire ends around each other. Cut the excess from the shorter wire (photo 13).
3. Using large rubberized round-nose pliers, wrap the wire, starting at the twisted end, around one jaw of the pliers to create the rounded shape of an earring loop (photo 14).
4. I also like to add a little flip at the end of the wire as a finishing detail. To create this effect, use large pliers to grip the tip of the wire and bend it up very slightly (photo 15).
5. Use wire cutters to cut the wire to the length you desire (photo 16).

In most cases, the components added to my earring loops (stones, bead links, etc.) are attached permanently, by slipping them on in step 1 after you've made the first loop. Once a loop is made, it will keep the design tightly fastened, but it also means that it can't be changed unless you cut through the twisted loop. See the project instructions for specific assembly directions for each set of earrings.

Working with Purchased Earring Findings

Rather than make your own ear wires, you can also use various types of prefabricated findings with rings or loops, such as ball-post earrings, lever-back earrings, traditional French ear wires, and more. You can also use ear clips, if your ears aren't pierced. Attaching stones to these findings is very simple. With chain-nose pliers, grasp the loop on the finding and twist very slightly to one side. Never pull the loop open; instead, gently twist it to one side. Then place the chain or a stone on the open loop and close, again using the chain-nose pliers. You can see how easy it is to substitute the findings as you wish when you make your own pieces of jewelry.

Working with Chain

Chain is one of the simplest materials to use in jewelry making. The toughest part will be deciding which type to use! After that, all you'll need to do is cut the chain and create your piece.

I have specified the lengths of chain you need for each design in the book. Rulers are helpful, of course, but be careful not to rely on them for determining the length of the chain. Instead, always make it a practice to count the links. I can't recommend this enough!

Counting links is of utmost importance when working with short paired lengths of chain, such as for earrings. The difference of even one small chain link will make your earring noticeably lopsided. While it may seem very tedious to count chain links, especially for longer pieces such as the City Nights necklace (page 114), it is much easier to count the links ahead of time than to fix a mistake.

Use a ruler to measure only the first length of chain, then count the links in that segment, and count all additional chain segments to make absolutely certain that each one has exactly the same number of links. After you determine the right length for the piece you are making, pull out your trusty wire cutters and snip.

For pieces that are made with long lengths of chain, you'll want to have the flexibility of making the chain exactly your desired length. This is another reason not to rely only on a ruler for measurement. Be sure to check the fit of a bracelet or necklace before cutting the chain. For example, I specify the number of links in the chain for the Charming bracelet (page 44) to make it easier for you to replicate the design.

To attach a chain to wire or a finding, slide one link of the chain (often an end link) onto a wire loop or finding. Generally, the chain is secured with wrapped wire.

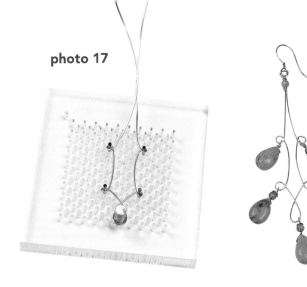

photo 17

Using Special Tools

Jigs are especially handy because they allow you to quickly create multiple wire designs, all of them identical. A jig is basically a flat surface with equidistant holes. You place pegs in these holes to form the desired pattern, and then you wrap wire around them to form a looped wire design (photo 17). Be sure to experiment with inexpensive wire until you're pleased with the results of your jig work, then switch to precious-metal wire to make your jewelry design.

A ring sizer is a keychain-like loop containing graduated steel rings in all sizes. You can determine which ring size to make by slipping these rings on and off your finger to find the best fit. I recommend always building rings one-half to one size larger than finger size, especially for wide rings.

A mandrel is a tool that is useful for determining ring sizes as well as for building a ring. Use a mandrel to hold the ring (photo 18) in place while you're working on it.

photo 18

Making Size Adjustments

Each set of project instructions in this book lists the finished size of the piece of jewelry. As a rule, the average length for necklaces is 16 inches (40.6 cm), while bracelets average 7 inches (17.8 cm), but there are many variations depending on the project and how it fits the person who will be wearing it. Another good option for deciding what length to make a piece is to measure some of your favorite jewelry and make your new piece the same length. If you're making jewelry for others, measure some of their pieces that have a similar design before you begin.

To make a piece larger or longer, simply add an additional stone or another few beads. If your project involves the use of chain, lengthen the segments of chain that are used in the design. Keep in mind that when you make a piece larger, you'll need additional materials, so remember this when you're preparing your shopping list.

For most necklaces, you have the option of making them longer by adding a toggle to the catch at the back of the necklace (page 22). I've included a toggle on several of my necklace designs, including Twilight (page 49), Dangle (page 68), and Fireworks (page 30).

For a different type of necklace, I've designed Duet (page 62) to fasten lariat-style in front. You can make this necklace longer simply by using a longer length of chain.

Bracelets, depending on their design, often present the greatest challenge when making size adjustments. To make them larger, you may need to add an extra stone, such as for Beyond (page 59), or add links to the chain

Toggle

segments used in the design, as in Charming (page 44) and Starburst (page 101). Sometimes a short toggle is a simple solution for lengthening bracelets.

For rings, as I wrote in the previous section, using a ring sizer and a mandrel will ensure that the band is the size you want it to be. For most pieces, you can adjust the size of the band without changing the design of the ring, such as for the Sea Bundle ring (page 108).

BEGINNER PROJECTS

SIMPLICITY

Lemon quartz and amethyst is a perfect combination for simple earrings that you can make in a jiffy.

Instructions

Finished size: 3¾ inches (9.5 cm)

Materials

2 lemon quartz nuggets, 15 mm

4 amethyst briolettes, 8 mm

7-inch (17.8 cm) length of 1-mm gold-filled chain

5-inch (12.7 cm) length of 22-gauge gold-filled wire

10-inch (25.4 cm) length of 26-gauge gold-filled wire

Tools

Chain-nose pliers

Round-nose pliers

Wire cutters

Large rubberized round-nose pliers

Ruler

Techniques

Making Twisted Wire Loop Links (page 20)

Making Earring Loops (page 24)

Make two

1. Cut the chain, making the following four segments: two 2-inch (5.1 cm) segments and two 1½-inch (3.8 cm) segments. Count the links to be sure the chain segments are the same length.

2. Slide one 8-mm amethyst briolette onto the 26-gauge wire, with one end extending ¾ inch (1.9 cm) from the hole. Bend both wires upward until they cross. Tightly twist the wires around once. Cut off the shorter wire end.

3. Hold the remaining wire with the round-nose pliers and loop around.

4. Slide the wire through the last link in one of the chain segments. Holding onto the loop with the chain-nose pliers, wrap the wire around the twist you made in step 2. Cut off the excess wire.

5. Repeat steps 2 through 4 three more times, until all four briolettes are attached to a length of chain.

6. Make another loop in the 26-gauge wire, ¾ inch (1.9 cm) from the end. Place two of the chain segments (one of each length) onto the wire so they hang from the loop. Hold the loop with the chain-nose pliers and twist the wires around to secure the chains in place. Cut off the shorter wire end and bend the longer wire up so it is centered over the loop (figure 1).

fig. 1

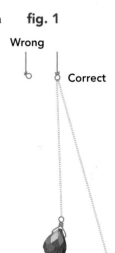

Wrong   Correct

7. Slide one 15-mm quartz nugget onto the wire and bend the wire 45°. Using the round-nose pliers, loop the wire around. Hold the loop with the chain-nose pliers and wrap the wire around to secure.

8. To make the earring loops, cut the 22-gauge wire into two pieces, each 2½ inches (6.4 cm) long. With the round-nose pliers, grip one piece of wire ¾ inch (1.9 cm) from the end and wrap to make a loop.

9. Slide this wire through the loop on top of the quartz nugget. Hold this new loop with the chain-nose pliers and wrap it around two times. Cut off the shorter wire end.

10. Using the rubberized round-nose pliers, clamp down on the wire right above the twist and bend the wire around the jaw of the pliers. Cut the wire to the desired length.

11. Using the chain-nose pliers, grasp the tip of the wire and bend it slightly upward to give the earring a finishing touch (page 24).

FIREWORKS

Finished size: 19 inches (48.3 cm);
longest dangle, 2¾ inches (7 cm)

Materials

13 citrine briolettes, 4 mm

22 peridot briolettes, 3 mm

22 apatite briolettes, 3 mm

5 gold-filled, ball-end head pins,
1½ inches (3.8 cm) long

13 gold-filled, ball-end head pins, 1 inch (2.5 cm) long

4 gold-filled beads, 3 mm

9 gold-filled beads, 2 mm

11 irregular gold rondelles, 4 mm

1 gold-filled lobster clasp

15-inch (38.1 cm) length of 1.5-mm gold-filled chain

2-inch (5.1 cm) length of 2.5-mm gold-filled chain
(for the toggle)

6-inch (15.2 cm) length of gold-filled 24-gauge wire

12-inch (30.5 cm) length of gold-filled 26-gauge wire

Tools

Chain-nose pliers, 2 pair

Round-nose pliers

Wire cutters

Ruler

Techniques

Making Twisted Wire Loop Links (page 20)

Making Catches and Clasps (page 22)

Working with Head Pins (page 23)

Instructions

1. Using the ruler and wire cutters, measure and then cut off a 3-inch (7.6 cm) segment from the 15-inch chain. Cut the remaining 12 inches (30.5 cm) to make the following segments: four 1½-inch (3.8 cm) segments, two 2½-inch (6.4 cm) segments, and one 1-inch (2.5 cm) segment.

2. Attach one of the 2½-inch (6.4 cm) segments to the 2-inch (5.1 cm) 2.5-mm toggle chain with a twisted loop link; using the round-nose pliers, make a loop ¾ inch (1.9 cm) from the end of the 24-gauge wire. Slide this loop onto the final link of the 2½-inch (6.4 cm) segment. Hold the loop with the chain-nose pliers and twist to secure. Cut off the shorter wire end.

3. Using the round-nose pliers, make a new loop in the wire, this time sliding it onto the end link of the toggle chain. Hold this second loop with the chain-nose pliers and wrap the wire around the twist you made in step 2.

4. With the 26-gauge wire, create a loop ¾ inch (1.9 cm) from the end with the round-nose pliers. Slide it onto the remaining end of the thinner necklace chain (not the toggle chain). Hold this loop with pliers and wrap the wires around to secure. Cut off the shorter wire end.

5. Slide onto this wire the stones for this first section, as follows: one 2-mm gold-filled bead, one 3-mm peridot briolette, one 4-mm irregular gold briolette, one 3-mm peridot briolette, and one 2-mm gold-filled bead.

6. After the beads are in place, bend the wire 45°. Use the round-nose pliers to make a new loop and slide a 1½-inch (3.8 cm) chain length onto this loop. Hold the loop with the chain-nose pliers and wrap the wire around to secure. Cut off the excess wire.

FIREWORKS

This necklace will light up the night with its sparkling gemstones clustered on an eye-catching dangle.

7. fig. 1

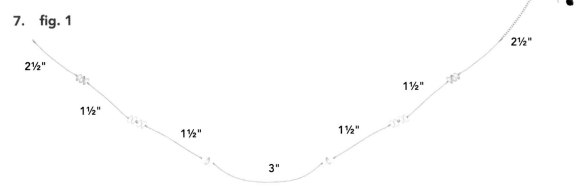

To work the remainder of the chain section of the necklace, repeat steps 4 through 6, following the pattern in figure 1, keeping the 3-inch (7.6 cm) chain segment in the middle. Following are the stone patterns used for the other sections on the chain: The first and sixth bead sections are as described in step 5; the second and fifth bead sections are two 3-mm apatite briolettes, one 2-mm gold-filled bead, and two 3-mm apatite briolettes; the third and fourth bead sections are one 4-mm citrine briolette, one 3-mm peridot briolette, and one citrine briolette.

8. Find the middle link of the central 3-inch chain segment. Using the 24-gauge wire and the round-nose pliers, make a new loop ¾ inch (1.9 cm) from the end of the wire. Slide the loop onto this middle link. Hold the loop using the chain-nose pliers and twist the wires around to secure. Cut off the shorter wire end.

9. Slide one 3-mm peridot briolette, one 4-mm irregular gold briolette, and one 3-mm peridot briolette onto the wire. Bend the wire 45°, loop it around on the round-nose pliers, and place the remaining 1-inch (2.5 cm) chain segment on this loop. Hold the loop with the chain-nose pliers and wrap the wire around to secure. Cut off the excess wire.

10. Take all 18 of the head pins, both 1½-inch (3.8 cm) and 1-inch (2.5 cm) lengths. Set aside one of each size for the closure of the necklace; the other 16 will be used to decorate the 1-inch (2.5 cm) hanging chain segment.

11. Begin by selecting one head pin and sliding two to four beads onto it. (For each head pin, combine the stones and gold-filled beads in a different order to create variety.) After the beads are in place, use the

fig. 2

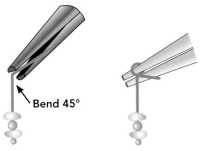

chain-nose pliers to bend the head pin about ⅜ inch (9.5 mm) from the top. Place the round-nose pliers above the bend and loop the wire around (figure 2).

12. Slide this head pin onto the wire loop from which the 1-inch (2.5 cm) chain length is hanging. Hold the loop with the chain-nose pliers and wrap the wire around to secure. (***Note:*** I strongly recommend using two pair of chain-nose pliers for this, one in each hand, because the wire length is very short and it is difficult to maneuver with your fingers.) Cut off the excess wire.

13. Repeat steps 11 and 12 until you've placed all 16 head pins along the links of the 1-inch (2.5 cm) chain. While working down the chain, spread out the placement of the four 1½-inch (3.8 cm) head pins among the twelve 1-inch (2.5 cm) head pins.

14. Begin working on the closure of the necklace. Select one of the head pins you reserved and repeat step 11. Place a few stones on it and slide it onto the bottom link of the toggle chain. Hold the loop with the chain-nose pliers and wrap the wire around to secure. Cut off the excess wire. Repeat for the remaining head pin, this time attaching it a few links up the toggle chain. Cut off the excess wire.

15. Attach the lobster clasp to the other end of the chain. Using the 24-gauge wire and round-nose pliers,

make a new loop. Slide the final link of the necklace chain onto this loop. Hold the loop with the chain-nose pliers and twist the wires to secure. Cut off the shorter wire end.

16. Bend the wire 45° and loop it again with the round-nose pliers. Slide the lobster clasp onto this loop. Hold the loop with the chain-nose pliers and wrap the wire around the twist you made in step 15. Cut off the excess wire.

RAINDROPS

Three lovely pearls drop gently on these simple earrings,
a versatile addition to your jewelry collection.

Instructions

Materials

6 white pearls (disks), 12 mm

6 sterling silver ball-end head pins,
1½ inches (3.8 cm) long

12-inch (30.5 cm) length of 1.5-mm
sterling silver chain

5-inch (12.7 cm) length of 22-gauge
sterling silver wire

Tools

Chain-nose pliers

Round-nose pliers

Wire cutters

Large rubberized round-nose pliers

Ruler

Techniques

Making Twisted Wire Loop Links
(page 20)

Making Earring Loops (page 24)

Make two

1. Cut the chain into segments as follows: two 1-inch (2.5 cm) segments, two 2-inch (5.1 cm) segments, and two 3-inch (7.6 cm) segments. (*Note:* It's extremely important when making earrings that the lengths of chain are identical. Be sure to count the links to make certain that they match; don't rely on measuring the chain with a ruler.) Keep the three different lengths paired together.

2. **fig. 1**

    Select a pearl and slide it onto a head pin. Bend the head pin 45° and use the round-nose pliers to loop it around one jaw of the pliers (figure 1).

3. Select one of the chain segments and place the last link on the loop you've just created on the head pin.

4. Hold the loop with the chain-nose pliers and wrap the wire around two or three times. Cut off the excess wire.

5. Repeat steps 2 through 4 until the six chain segments are each attached to a pearl. Place the chains in two groups containing one of each length.

6. To make the earring loop, first cut the 5-inch (12.7 cm) length of 22-gauge wire in half to make two 2½-inch (6.4 cm) lengths, one for each earring. Using the round-nose pliers, grip one of the wires ¾ inch (1.9 cm) from the end. Wrap the wire around the jaw of the pliers to form a loop. Then place all three chains (shortest to longest or vice versa) onto the wire so they hang from the loop.

7. Hold the loop with the chain-nose pliers and wrap the wires around two times. Cut off the shorter wire end.

8. Using the rubberized round-nose pliers, hold the wire just above the twist and wrap the wire around to form the earring loop. Cut the wire to your desired length. Use these same pliers to gently squeeze the earring loop to flatten and straighten it.

9. For a final touch, use the chain-nose pliers to grasp the tip of the wire and bend it slightly upward (page 24).

GRAPEVINE

For a special night out, embellish yourself with this dramatic necklace with large amethyst focal beads.

Instructions

Finished size: 15½ inches (39.4 cm);
longer dangle, 4 inches (10.2 cm)

Materials

2 extra-large amethyst drops, 40 mm

3 amethyst nuggets, 20 mm

4 amethyst beads, 10 mm

2 sterling silver beads, 3 mm

2 sterling silver ball-end head pins,
2½ inches (6.4 cm) long

1 sterling silver lobster clasp

48-inch (122 cm) length of 1.5-mm
sterling silver chain

15-inch (38.1 cm) length of 24-gauge
sterling silver wire

Tools

Chain-nose pliers

Round-nose pliers

Wire cutters

Large rubberized round-nose pliers

Ruler

Techniques

Making Twisted Wire Loop Links
(page 20)

Making Catches and Clasps (page 22)

1. Slide one 3-mm silver bead and one large 40-mm amethyst drop onto a 2½-inch (6.4 cm) ball-end head pin.

2. Bend the top of the ball-end pin 45°. Hold the pin with the round-nose pliers and bend the pin around the pliers. Place this loop onto the first link of the silver chain. Using the chain-nose pliers, hold the loop and twist the wire to secure the silver bead, the amethyst drop, and the silver chain link.

3. Cut the chain, leaving a ½-inch (1.3 cm) length attached.

4. Repeat steps 1 and 2 with the second 40-mm amethyst drop, this time measuring and cutting the silver chain to leave a 2-inch (5.1 cm) length attached.

5. With the 24-gauge wire, use the round-nose pliers to make a loop about ¾ inch (1.9 cm) from the end. Place both chain ends attached to the two large amethyst drops onto this loop. Hold the loop with the chain-nose pliers and twist to secure. Cut off the shorter wire end.

6. Slide the 24-gauge wire through one 20-mm amethyst nugget. Bend the wire at the top about 45°. Using the round-nose pliers, bend the wire around to secure.

7. Cut the chain to make six segments in the following lengths: two short segments each 1½ inches (3.8 cm), two medium segments each 1¾ inches (4.4 cm), and two long segments each 2 inches (5.1 cm). (*Note:* I highly recommend counting the links before cutting the chain to make sure that each pair of chain segments is exactly the same.)

8. Place the six chain segments onto the looped wire in the following order: long, medium, short, short, medium, long.

9. After all of the chain segments are in place on the wire loop, hold the loop with the chain-nose pliers and wrap the wire around to secure all pieces in place.

Designer's Tip

When working with multiple chains that are attached together, make sure the chains don't tangle or twist by keeping all of the chain links facing the same direction. I recommend letting the chains hang while working with them so you'll be able to see each chain. Careful attention to the details makes a big difference in the overall appearance of fine jewelry.

10. Cut twelve ¾-inch (1.9 cm) chain segments. This is worth repeating: Count the links before cutting to make sure all of them are exactly the same length.

11. Make a new wire loop using the round-nose pliers. Select three consecutive chains from one side, choosing one of each length: long, medium, and short. Place the three chains onto the loop.

12. Hold this loop with the chain-nose pliers and twist the wire around to secure. Cut off the shorter wire end.

13. **fig. 1**

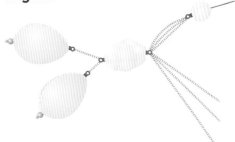

Slide one 10-mm amethyst bead onto the wire (figure 1). Bend the wire 45°, hold it with the round-nose pliers, and loop it around.

14. Place three ¾-inch (1.9 cm) chain segments onto the loop. Hold the loop with the chain-nose pliers and wrap the wire around to secure. Cut off the excess wire.

15. Make a new loop in the wire with the round-nose pliers. Place all three ends of the ¾-inch (1.9 cm) chain segments onto the loop. Using the chain-nose pliers, twist the wire around to secure. Cut off the shorter wire end.

16. Slide a 20-mm amethyst nugget onto the wire. Bend the wire 45° and use the round-nose pliers to loop it. Place three ¾-inch (1.9 cm) chain segments onto the loop and use the chain-nose pliers to wrap the wire to secure. Cut off the excess wire.

17. Make a new loop in the wire using the round-nose pliers. Place three ¾-inch (1.9 cm) chain segments onto the loop and twist the wires around to secure. Cut off the shorter wire end.

18. Place another 10-mm amethyst bead onto this wire. Bend the wire 45° and use the round-nose pliers to loop the wire around to secure.

19. Cut six 3-inch (7.6 cm) chain segments. Place three of them onto the loop you've just made. Hold the loop with the chain-nose pliers and wrap the wire around to secure. Cut off the excess wire.

20. Pick up the three remaining chain segments (one each of short, medium, and long) from step 11. Repeat steps 11 through 19 to make the other side of the necklace.

21. You're now ready to attach the lobster clasp to the back of the necklace. Using the 24-gauge wire and round-nose pliers, make a new loop. Place the three chains from one side of the necklace onto this loop. Hold the loop with the chain-nose pliers and twist the wires to secure them. Cut off the shorter wire end.

22. Bend the wire 45° and loop it again with the round-nose pliers. Slide the lobster clasp onto this loop and hold the loop with the chain-nose pliers. Wrap the wire around the twist you made in step 21 and cut off the excess wire.

23. On the other side of the necklace, make the hook for the clasp. Make a new loop in the wire. Place all three chains onto this loop and twist the wires to secure. Cut off the shorter wire end.

24. Grip the wire with the rubberized round-nose pliers and loop it around. Then hold the loop with these pliers and wrap the wire around the twist you made in step 23. Cut off the excess wire.

Brightly colored briolettes dangle from a single chain for jaunty earrings that work for both day and evening wear.

RAINBOW

RAINBOW

Finished size: 3⅝ inches (9.2 cm)

Materials

3 rose quartz briolettes (round), 6 mm

4 green grossular garnet briolettes (round), 6 mm

4 honey jasper briolettes (round), 4 mm

3 cherry quartz briolettes (round), 6 mm

3 light green chalcedony briolettes (flat), 8 mm

4 periwinkle blue chalcedony briolettes (flat), 8 mm

3 blue chalcedony briolettes (flat), 8 mm

2 sterling silver French ear wires with loop and coil

5½-inch (14 cm) length of 1.5-mm sterling silver chain

24-inch (61 cm) length of 26-gauge sterling silver wire

Tools

Chain-nose pliers

Round-nose pliers

Wire cutters

Ruler

Techniques

Making Twisted Wire Loop Links (page 20)

Working with Purchased Earring Findings (page 24)

Designer's Notes

For this design, I used purchased ear wires instead of making them. If you choose to do the same, use the chain-nose pliers to bend the loop slightly to one side to open it. Slide the chain onto the loop and carefully press the loop back into place with the chain-nose pliers.

I've found that it works best to hang an earring while I'm working on it so I can see how the stones are falling and check the placement balance, particularly with this design. Be sure to attach the briolettes to opposite sides of the chain as you work your way up.

Instructions

Make two

1. Cut the chain into two segments of 2¾ inches (7 cm) each. Count the links to make sure that the length of each chain segment is exactly the same. Place one chain on the loop of the ear wire as described in the Designer's Notes.

2. The technique for making these earrings is to start at the bottom of the chain and place one briolette on the lowest link. Count up about six links and place the second briolette (figure 1). As you move up the chain, continue to attach briolettes, but each time reduce the number of links between them. By the time you reach the top of the chain, you will be placing a stone on each link.

fig. 1

3. To attach a stone, slide the 26-gauge wire through one bead, letting about ¾ inch (1.9 cm) of the wire extend through the other end. Bend both wire ends up until they cross at the top of the briolette. Twist the two ends together to secure. Cut off the shorter wire end.

4. Using the round-nose pliers, make a loop in the wire immediately above the twist. Run the wire through one of the links in the chain until the loop hangs from the link. Using the chain-nose pliers, hold the loop and wrap the wire around the twist you made in step 3. Cut off the excess wire.

5. Repeat steps 3 and 4 with the remaining briolettes, randomly placing 12 stones on each earring.

SAHARA

The ultimate in a piece of simple but versatile jewelry, this design is one long strand that can be worn as a necklace, a bracelet, or even a belt.

SAHARA

Finished size: 84½ inches (214.6 cm)

Materials

32 amber beads (organic shape), 8 mm

27 apatite beads (organic shape), 8 mm

17 brushed gold beads, 8 mm

2 gold-filled ball-end head pins,
    1 inch (2.5 cm) long

52½-inch (133.4 cm) length of 1.5-mm
    gold-filled chain

68-inch (172.7 cm) length of 24-gauge
    gold-filled wire

Tools

Chain-nose pliers

Round-nose pliers

Wire cutters

Ruler

Techniques

Making Twisted Wire Loop Links
    (page 20)

Instructions

1. Select a head pin and slide one 8-mm brushed gold bead onto it. Bend the wire 45° and use the round-nose pliers to loop it around. Slide the loop onto the bottom link of the chain. Hold the loop with the chain-nose pliers and wrap the wire around to secure. Cut off the excess wire.

2. Cut the chain about 1½ inches (3.8 cm) from the attached head pin.

3. Make a loop using the 24-gauge wire and round-nose pliers. Slide this loop onto the end of the 1½-inch (3.8 cm) segment of chain. Hold the loop with the chain-nose pliers and twist the wires around to secure. Cut off the shorter wire end.

4. Slide one 8-mm amber bead, one 8-mm apatite bead, and another amber bead onto the wire (figure 1). Bend the wire 45°. Use the round-nose pliers to make a loop and slide the length of chain onto this loop. Hold this loop with the chain-nose pliers and wrap the wire around to secure. Cut off the excess wire.

fig. 1

5. Cut the chain to 1 to 2 inches (2.5 to 5.1 cm) in length. Repeat steps 3 and 4 using a different set of stones, such as one amber bead and one brushed gold bead.

6. Continue adding twisted wire bead links and chain as in steps 3 and 4, varying your stone choices each time, not only in the order of stones but also the number, using one, two, or three stones. This design works best when the segments of chain are between 1 and 2 inches (2.5 and 5.1 cm) in length.

7. After you've used all of the chain, select the last head pin and one final stone. Slide this stone onto the head pin, bend the pin 45°, and loop it around using the round-nose pliers.

8. Place this loop onto the final link in the chain. Hold the loop with the chain-nose pliers and wrap the wire around to secure. Cut off the excess wire.

Finished size: 7⅛ inches (18.1 cm)

Materials

9 white pearls (disks), 10 mm

6 soft pink pearls (disks), 12 mm

3 gray pearls (disks), 12 mm

18 sterling silver ball-end head pins,
   1 inch (2.5 cm) long

1 sterling silver lobster clasp

6½-inch (16.5 cm) length of 1.5-mm
   sterling silver chain

2-inch (5.1 cm) length of 24-gauge
   sterling silver wire

Tools

Chain-nose pliers

Round-nose pliers

Wire cutters

Large rubberized round-nose pliers

Techniques

Making Twisted Wire Loop Links
   (page 20)

Making Catches and Clasps (page 22)

Designer's Tip

For a project such as this one that is made
with a long length of chain, I recommend
not cutting the chain to the specified
length until you've worked to the other
end. All chains are slightly different,
and you'll want to have the flexibility
of cutting the chain to exactly the right
length for the bracelet after you've
attached all of the beads or stones.

1. Using round-nose pliers, make a loop in the wire by holding it about ¾ inch (1.9 cm) from the end and wrapping the wire around. Slide the clasp onto this loop. Hold the loop with chain-nose pliers and twist the wires around to secure the clasp. Cut off the shorter wire end. Using round-nose pliers, bend the wire 45° and create a new loop. Slide one end of the chain onto it, holding it with the chain-nose pliers, and wrap the wire around to secure. Cut off the excess wire.

2. Select a 12-mm pearl and slide it onto a ball-end head pin. With the pearl in place, bend the head pin 45°. Hold it with round-nose pliers and loop it. Slide the head pin loop through the second link in the chain, adjacent to the one connected to the clasp. With the chain-nose pliers, hold the loop on the head pin and wrap it around to secure the loop. Cut off the excess wire. The first pearl is now in place (figure 1).

fig. 1

3. Slide a 10-mm pearl onto a head pin. Bend the head pin and loop it around as done in step 2. String it onto one of the links in the chain, six to eight links from the previous pearl. Wrap the head pin around and cut off the excess. *Note:* From this point on, always leave an odd number of links between each pearl. Make sure the pearls fall evenly from the chain by attaching each on the same side of the chain link.

4. Add the remaining pearls using the method in step 3. Alternate the placement of the 10-mm white pearls with the 12-mm pink and gray pearls as desired. Wrap the bracelet around your wrist to make sure the chain length is a good fit. Keep in mind that it will be slightly longer after you attach the catch for the clasp. Add extra pearls to create more length, if necessary. Cut the chain to your desired length.

5. Make a catch for the clasp by making a new loop in the wire. Slide this loop through the link following your last hanging pearl. Hold the loop with the chain-nose pliers and twist the wires around to secure. Cut off the shorter wire end.

6. Using the rubberized round-nose pliers, wrap the wire to form a large loop. Hold this loop firmly in the same tool and wrap the wire around the twist made in step 6 to secure. Cut off the excess wire.

CHARMING

Craft a truly elegant charm bracelet with disk-shaped pearls in soft colors of white, pink, and gray.

COUNTLESS

Create this easily adaptable bracelet using purple and green gemstones, or select other color and stone combinations to match your mood.

Instructions

Materials

18 amethyst beads (round), 8 mm

12 peridot beads (round), 6 mm

13 peridot beads (oval), 8 mm

16 gold-filled beads, 3 mm

1 gold-filled four-strand slide clasp

55-inch (139.7 cm) length of 3.5-mm gold-filled chain

88-inch (223.5 cm) length of 24-gauge gold-filled wire

Tools

Chain-nose pliers

Round-nose pliers

Wire cutters

Ruler

Techniques

Making Twisted Wire Loop Links (page 20)

Working with Catches and Clasps (page 22)

1. Separate the two slide clasp pieces while making the bracelet, always being careful to attach each strand to the correct loop. Begin by making wire loop links to attach the chain to the slide clasp. Loop the 24-gauge wire around the round-nose pliers about ¾ inch (1.9 cm) from the end of the wire. To make the loop larger, wrap the wire around the pliers at a thicker part of the jaws. After you've made the first loop, thread the slide clasp onto it. Also place the chain on this loop before wrapping the wire around to secure it. Hold this loop with the chain-nose pliers and twist the wire around to secure. Cut off the shorter wire end.

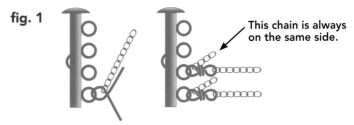

fig. 1

This chain is always on the same side.

Note: When placing the chain on the other three wire loops that will be connected to the slide clasp, always be sure to place the chain on the same side of the loop to maintain consistency (figure 1).

2. Hold the remaining wire with the round-nose pliers and loop it again. Cut the attached chain to about ½ inch (1.3 cm) in length so that you can attach a new piece. Slip a new chain length onto the other wire loop. Hold the loop with the chain-nose pliers and wrap the wire around the twist you made in step 1. Cut off the excess wire.

3. Now for the fun part! This bracelet requires you to experiment. The stones are randomly placed throughout, which means the length of the chain between each stone is completely up to you. For the bracelet shown, I varied the length of chain between the stones from a single link to about 1 inch (2.5 cm).

4. Attach a stone or stones (I don't recommend more then two) to the end of the first chain by making a loop in the wire about ¾ inch (1.9 cm) from the end. Attach this loop to the end of the chain. Hold this loop with the chain-nose pliers and twist the wires around to secure. Place a stone or stones onto the wire, bend the wire 45°, and loop it again using the round-nose pliers. Attach a new length of chain onto this loop and hold the loop with the chain-nose pliers. Wrap the wire around to secure and cut off the excess wire.

5. fig. 2

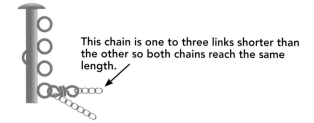

This chain is one to three links shorter than the other so both chains reach the same length.

Repeat steps 3 and 4 on both chains until you reach the length you need and are ready to attach it to the other half of the slide clasp. *Note:* The top chain on the first end should remain the top chain on this end, too. Therefore, the top chain will need to be slightly longer because it needs to reach the first loop of the wire link (figure 2).

6. Repeat step 1 but in reverse, attaching the bottom (shorter) end to the looped wire first. Twist it to secure. Using the round-nose pliers, bend the wire a second time and slide it through the slide clasp. Place the second chain on this same loop. Hold

the loop with the chain-nose pliers. Wrap the wire around the twist you just made and cut off the excess wire. You've finished the first length of the bracelet.

7. Repeat steps 1 through 6 three more times to complete the bracelet. As you work, study your completed sections to make sure you're not placing similar stones too close together. Plan the length of the chain segments so the stones are interspersed throughout.

TWILIGHT

Three graceful strands of soft blue and gray gemstones provide the perfect setting for this eye-catching blistered pearl pendant.

TWILIGHT

Finished size: 19 inches (48.3 cm)

Materials

1 blistered pearl pendant, 45 mm

10 light blue chalcedony nuggets, 18 mm

15 gray pearls, 8 mm

6 light blue crystals, 12 mm

7 light blue crystals, 10 mm

1 sterling silver lobster clasp

1 sterling silver ball-end head pin, 1 inch (2.5 cm) long

30-inch (76.2 cm) length of 1.5-mm sterling silver chain

2½-inch (5.1 cm) length of 2.5-mm sterling silver chain (for the toggle)

55-inch (139.7 cm) length of 24-gauge sterling silver wire

Tools

Chain-nose pliers

Round-nose pliers

Wire cutters

Ruler

Techniques

Making Twisted Wire Loop Links (page 20)

Making Catches and Clasps (page 22)

Instructions

1. The three strands of this necklace should be approximately 14 inches (35.6 cm), 15½ inches (39.4 cm), and 17 inches (43.2 cm) long, respectively. While working on each strand, keep a ruler handy for measuring your work as needed.

2. Begin work on the 14-inch (35.6 cm) strand. Make a twisted wire loop, using the round-nose pliers to hold the 24-gauge wire about ¾ inch (1.9 cm) from the end. Place one end of the 30-inch (76.2 cm), 1.5-mm silver chain onto the loop. Hold the loop with the round-nose pliers and twist the wires together. Cut off the shorter wire end. Cut the chain so a length of about 1½ inches (3.8 cm) of chain remains connected to the wire loop.

3. Slide one 8-mm gray pearl onto the wire. Use the round-nose pliers to bend the wire 45°, and then wrap it around. Place one end of the remaining 1.5-mm chain onto this loop. Using the chain-nose pliers, hold the loop and wrap it around to secure. Cut off the excess wire and trim the chain to a length of about 1 inch (2.5 cm).

4. Make a new loop in the wire, place it onto the end of the 1-inch (2.5 cm) piece of chain, and twist the wire around with the chain-nose pliers. Slide on one 10-mm light blue crystal, followed by another 8-mm gray pearl. Again bend the wire 45°, loop it around on the round-nose pliers, and attach it to another chain length about 1½ inches (3.8 cm) long. Once the chain is hanging from the loop, hold the loop with the chain-nose pliers and wrap the wire around to secure. Cut off the excess wire. Make a new wire loop at the end of this chain.

5. Attach an 18-mm chalcedony nugget to the wire. Before continuing to make the strand, pause for a moment to hold this to your neck to make sure you are pleased with how the chain and beads are coming together. Once you've added another length of chain, follow by perhaps adding a 12-mm light blue crystal bead, varying between the 10- and 12-mm crystal beads and gray pearls as you work.

6. Keep working all the way around in this manner until you've completed the 14-inch (35.6 cm) strand. Set aside this strand.

Nugget and Bead Placement

The design and construction of this necklace is very free once you determine the placement of the ten 18-mm chalcedony nuggets. These need to be placed on the three strands somewhat symmetrically (but not perfectly) so the necklace falls correctly (figure 1).

Then you can place the smaller beads in a random fashion, allowing 1 to 2 inches (2.5 to 5.1 cm) of chain between the various elements. I recommend that you periodically hold the unfinished piece to your neck so you can see how the necklace is progressing. You may want to make changes to the length of the chain segments, adjusting them to be longer or shorter, or to the selection and placement of the stones.

fig. 1

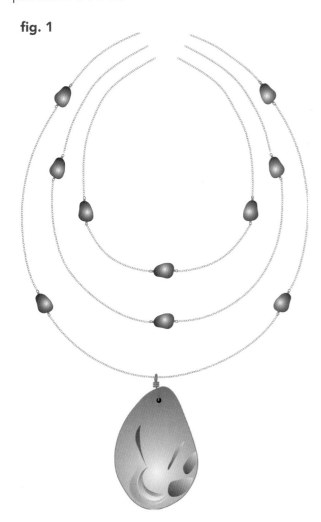

7. Begin the 15½-inch (39.4 cm) strand, working in the same manner of attaching the beads and chain as for the first strand, using steps 2 through 6 as a guide. To see how it falls, hold the chain ends of the first and second strands together. It's important to frequently evaluate how the strands fall together so you can balance the bead placement and chain lengths as you work.

8. For the third strand, the blistered pearl pendant will be attached in the center. If you follow the suggested lengths, the center of the 17-inch (43.2 cm) strand will be 8½ inches (21.6 cm) from the end. To attach the pendant, slide the wire through the bead hole, allowing ¾ inch (1.9 cm) to pass through. Bend both ends up. Bend the two wires again at the top

fig. 2

so they cross tightly and twist them around to secure (figure 2). Cut off the shorter wire end.

9. Using the round-nose pliers, make a loop in the wire and slide it to the 8½-inch (21.6 cm) mark on the third strand of the necklace. With the chain-nose pliers, hold the loop and wrap the wire around the twist you made in step 8. Cut off the excess wire.

10. Make the third strand in the same manner of attaching the beads and chain as for the first strand, using steps 2 through 6 as a guide.

11. After you've completed all three strands of the necklace, use the round-nose pliers to make a new loop in the wire. Place all three chain ends onto this loop. Hold the loop with the chain-nose pliers and twist the wires around to secure. Cut off the shorter wire end.

12. Use the round-nose pliers to loop the wire around again. Place the lobster clasp onto this loop. Hold the loop with the chain-nose pliers and wrap the wire around the twist you made in step 11. Cut off the excess wire.

13. Pick up the other end of the necklace and place all three of these chain ends onto a new wire loop made with the round-nose pliers. Repeat the same process as in step 12 of twisting the wires around and making a new loop.

14. Place the 2½ inches (5.1 cm) of 2.5-mm silver chain onto the loop you made in step 13.

15. Hold the wire loop with the chain-nose pliers and wrap the wire around the twist you made in step 13. Cut off the excess wire.

16. Use the 1-inch (2.5 cm) head pin to add a detail on the end of the toggle. Slide a 10-mm light blue crystal bead onto the head pin. Bend the wire of the head pin 45°, hold it with the round-nose pliers, and then loop it around. Attach the loop to the last link in the toggle chain. Holding the loop with the chain-nose pliers, wrap the wire around to secure, and then cut off the excess wire.

BALLOONS

Your hands will be awash in pearls with this glamorous design.
The construction is so easy you'll want to make several of them.

Instructions

Ring size: 6½

Materials

16 white pearls, 8 mm

56 sterling silver beads, 3 mm

2 sterling silver four-hole separator bars

4 sterling silver crimping beads

16-inch (40.6 cm) length of clear elastic cord, 0.7 mm diameter

Tools

Chain-nose pliers

Needle threader

Ruler

Scissors

Glue

Techniques

Using Special Tools (ring sizer, page 25)

1. With scissors, cut the 16-inch (40.8 cm) clear elastic cord into four 4-inch (10.2 cm) segments.

2. Slide four 8-mm pearls to the middle of one 4-inch (10.2 cm) length of cord. To make the job easier, use the needle threader; slide the wire of the needle threader through the hole of the bead, and then slip a very short piece of elastic cord, about ⅛ inch (3 mm), through the needle threader's wire loop. Carefully pull the needle threader with the elastic cord back through the bead. The smaller the bead holes, the more this technique will come in handy.

3. **fig. 1**

Place a 3-mm sterling silver bead on both sides of the group of pearls. Then add to both sides a separator bar and six 3-mm sterling silver beads (figure 1).

4. Add one crimping bead to one end of the cord, and then slide the other cord end through the other side of the bead (you may need to use the needle threader). Carefully pull on the two cord ends (figure 2) to bring the beads smoothly into place.

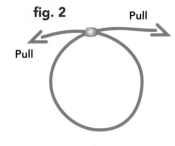

fig. 2   Pull   Pull

5. Use the chain-nose pliers to clamp down tightly on the crimping bead. After the cords are secure, cut off the excess on both sides.

6. Repeat steps 2 through 5 three more times, using all the holes in the separator bars to create the four strands of the ring.

7. Add a touch of glue to each of the crimping beads to secure the elastic cord.

Designer's Tip

These instructions and the listed materials for making the project are for a size 6½ ring. Depending on your ring size, you may need to add or subtract 3-mm silver beads. This may require some trial and error before you get the size and the number of beads exactly right, but the good news is that elastic cord is inexpensive. If you find you have the wrong fit, just cut the cord and try it again until you get it right. Also keep in mind that this ring consists of four strands around your finger, making it a wide ring. The wider the ring, the larger the size needs to be, so complete a minimum of three strands before checking the fit.

LILY

Instructions

Finished size: 1⅛ inch (2.8 cm)

Materials

2 rose quartz briolettes, 6 mm

2 green grossular garnet briolettes, 6 mm

2 honey jasper briolettes, 4 mm

Pink and purple seed beads

2 pink clay lilies with wire stems

2 gold-filled ball-post earrings with rings

2 gold-filled ball-end head pins, 2 inches (5.1 cm) long

1-inch (2.5 cm) length of 1.5-mm gold-filled chain

9-inch (22.9 cm) length of 26-gauge gold-filled wire

Tools

Chain-nose pliers

Round-nose pliers

Wire cutters

Ruler

Techniques

Making Twisted Wire Loop Links (page 20)

Working with Head Pins (page 23)

Instructions

Make two

1. Cut the 1-inch (2.5 cm) length of chain into two segments, each ½ inch (1.3 cm) long.

2. Using the chain-nose pliers, bend the ring on the ball-post earring slightly to the side. (*Note:* Always open these loops to the side so as not to weaken the loop.) Place one end of the ½-inch (1.3 cm) chain on the ring. Close the ring with the chain-nose pliers.

3. Slide the 26-gauge wire through one of the quartz briolettes, with ¾ inch (1.9 cm) of the wire extending out the other side. Bend up both wire ends until they cross tightly, and twist them around once to secure. Cut off the shorter wire end.

4. Using the round-nose pliers, loop the other wire end around. Slide the loop onto one of the chain links and, using the chain-nose pliers, wrap the wire around the twisted part. Cut off the excess.

5. Repeat steps 3 and 4 two more times to add a garnet and a jasper briolette, ending up with three different stones on the chain, and spacing out the three as much as possible.

6. Working with the lily, cut the wire stem to about 1 inch (2.5 cm) in length. Bend the wire stem into a curve and slide it through one of the chain links between two of the briolettes.

Designer's Tips

The clay lilies used in this earring design can be found in the wedding section of most craft and party stores. If you don't find the color you want, paint them with nail polish, letting them dry overnight before using them.

Be sure to choose a chain with links that are wide enough for the stems of the clay lilies to pass through them in step 6.

LILY

Small clay lilies provide a floral accent to the cluster of briolettes, giving a unique touch to this pair of pastel earrings.

7. Using the round-nose pliers, wrap the top of the wire stem around once or twice. This is all that's needed to hold the lily in place.

8. **fig. 1**   **fig. 2**

Twirl the head pins using the following technique. Wrap the pin around one jaw of the round-nose pliers by taking hold of the ball-end of the pin and twirling it around (figure 1). To continue the twist, release the pliers, rotate the pin slightly, grab on with the pliers again, and twist. Because the pliers are tapered, you'll need to be careful not to taper your twist. So to keep it even, flip the head pin when it is halfway done and continue wrapping it around the jaw. Leave a straight length of ¾ inch (1.9 cm) at the end (figure 2).

9. Select the seed beads and slide them onto the curled head pin, alternating the colors on the two earrings. Stop when you reach the straight part of the pin.

10. Attach the twirled head pin to the chain. Using the round-nose pliers, hold the straight end of the head pin and wrap it around to form a loop. Slide this loop onto one of the chain links between two briolettes. Hold the loop with the chain-nose pliers and wrap the wire around to secure. Cut off the excess wire.

BEYOND

Five lovely stones form the focal elements of this elegant bracelet, which is made with a delicate chain and simple wire loops.

Finished size: 7½ inches (19 cm)

Materials

3 black lace agate beads (round disks), 23 mm

2 black lace agate beads (oval disks), 18 mm

6 white howlite beads, 5 mm

2 sterling silver ball-end head pins, 2 inches (5.1 cm) long

2 sterling silver ball-end head pins, 1 inch (2.5 cm) long

1 sterling silver figure-eight lobster clasp

8-inch (20.3 cm) length of 1.5-mm sterling silver chain

14-inch (35.6 cm) length of 24-gauge sterling silver wire

Tools

Chain-nose pliers

Round-nose pliers

Wire cutters

Large rubberized round-nose pliers

Ruler

Techniques

Making Twisted Wire Loop Links (page 20)

Working with Head Pins (page 23)

Instructions

1. Make a twisted wire loop, using the round-nose pliers to hold the 24-gauge wire about ¾ inch (1.9 cm) from the end. Bend the wire around the pliers. Slide the silver clasp onto this loop. Now hold the loop with the chain-nose pliers and twist the wires around each other to secure. Cut off the shorter wire end.

2. Place one 5-mm howlite bead on the wire. Bend the wire 45° and make a new loop using the round-nose pliers. Use the chain-nose pliers to hold this loop, and then wrap the wire around itself to complete. Cut off the excess wire.

3. Create a new loop with the wire as in step 1. Slip this loop through the closed loop made at the end of the 5-mm howlite bead. Hold the loop with the chain-nose pliers and twist the wire again to secure it. Cut off the shorter wire end.

4. Slide a 23-mm agate bead onto the wire. Bend the wire and make a new loop.

5. It's very important for this project that each of the eight chain segments has exactly the same number of links. I highly recommend measuring only the first 1-inch (2.5 cm) segment, then counting the links for the other seven before cutting them. With this method of counting links, instead of measuring the segments with a ruler, you'll be sure to have identical lengths of chain. Slide two 1-inch (2.5 cm) segments of chain onto the wire so they hang from the loop formed in step 4. Hold this new loop with the round-nose pliers and wrap the wire around to secure it. Cut off the excess wire.

6. Select one 2-inch (5.1 cm) ball-end head pin and slide one 5-mm howlite bead onto it. Place one of the chains you've just strung plus another loose chain segment onto the head pin. Add one 18-mm agate bead. Place the second chain segment onto the end of the head pin and add another segment of loose chain (figure 1).

fig. 1

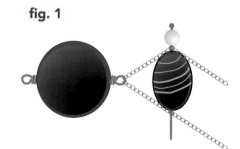

7. Bend the end of the ball-end head pin in step 6 with the round-nose pliers, make a loop, and wrap it around to secure the two beads and chain segments. Cut off the excess from the head pin.

8. Select a 1-inch (2.5 cm) ball-end head pin and slide on one 5-mm howlite bead. With the round-nose pliers, bend the head pin, make a loop, and place this loop onto the closed loop you just formed at the bottom of the 2-inch (5.1 cm) ball-end head pin in step 7. Use the chain-nose pliers to hold this loop and wrap the length of the head pin around itself. Cut off the excess from the head pin.

9. Make a new wire loop and place both of the loose chain segments that you attached in step 6 onto the loop. Wrap the wire to secure. Cut off the shorter wire end. Slide a 23-mm agate bead onto the wire, bend the wire, and make a loop.

10. Place the fifth and sixth chain segments onto the loop formed in step 9 and twist the wire to secure. Cut off the excess wire.

11. Repeat steps 6 through 9, adding the remaining stones to arrive at the other end of the bracelet. Loop the wire at the end of the 23-mm agate bead, bend it around using the chain-nose pliers, and cut off the excess wire.

12. Make a twisted wire loop and attach it to the loop at the end of the 23-mm agate bead. Slide the last howlite bead onto the wire; bend the wire 45°. Make a loop with the round-nose pliers. Hold the loop with the chain-nose pliers and wrap the wire around to secure.

13. To finish the bracelet, make a catch for the clasp with wire. Make a small wire loop using the round-nose pliers. Slide it through the last loop and wrap to secure. Cut off the shorter wire end.

14. Using the large rubberized round-nose pliers, hold the wire and bend it around to form a large loop. Hold the loop you've created with these same pliers and wrap the wire around the twist you made in step 13. Cut off the excess wire.

A rich cluster of gemstones is attached to both ends of a long chain, creating this luxe lariat necklace.

DUET

Instructions

Finished size: 36⅞ inches (93.6 cm)

Materials

2 moss quartz drops, 25 mm

7 jade beads, 5 mm

9 gray pearls (oval), 7 mm

8 green seed beads

9 sterling silver beads, 3 mm

6 sterling silver beads, 2 mm

2 sterling silver ball-end head pins,
    1½ inches (3.8 cm) long

34-inch (86.4 cm) length of 2-mm sterling
    silver chain

40-inch (101.6 cm) length of 26-gauge
    sterling silver wire

Tools

Chain-nose pliers

Round-nose pliers

Wire cutters

Techniques

Making Twisted Wire Loop Links
    (page 20)

Working with Head Pins (page 23)

1. Select the head pins, two 25-mm quartz drops, two 3-mm sterling silver beads, and the chain.

2. Slide one 3-mm bead and one quartz drop onto a head pin. Bend the head pin 45° and loop it around using the round-nose pliers. Attach it onto the end link in the chain by holding the wire loop with the chain-nose pliers, and then wrapping the wire around to secure. Cut off the excess wire (figure 1).

fig. 1

3. Repeat step 2 for the other end of the chain.

4. Separate the remaining beads and pearls to make two similar groups to attach to the two ends of the necklace. For this design, I've balanced the number of stones on the two ends, but the groups are not identical. I placed four 5-mm jade beads on one side and three on the other, and four 7-mm gray pearls on one side and five on the other, and so forth. In assembling the necklace, you can follow this example for bead placement or choose your own.

5. Use the 26-gauge wire to make eye pins for the detailed bead extensions. With the round-nose pliers, hold the tip of the wire. Twirl the wire around one and one-half times to make a loop (figure 2). Keep the pliers placed through the hole, but rotate them so the outer jaw is now on the straight wire. Bend the straight wire 45° to center the loop (figure 3).

fig. 2

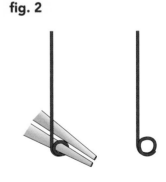

fig. 3

6. Slide one or two beads onto the wire. ***Note:*** Switch the bead combinations on every head pin to create variety. For example, make one head pin with one jade bead only, a second head pin with one 3-mm silver bead and one jade bead, and a third head pin with one jade bead, one seed bead, and one 2-mm silver bead.

7. After the beads on the head pin are in place, bend the wire 45°, loop it around using the round-nose pliers, and slide this loop onto a link in the chain immediately above the 25-mm quartz drop.

8. Hold this loop with the chain-nose pliers and wrap the wire around to secure. Cut off the excess wire.

9. To attach the oval pearls, you won't need to make a head pin. Instead, slide the wire through the pearl with ¾ inch (1.9 cm) extending out the other side. Bend both wire ends up until they cross tightly. Twist the two wires together one and one-half times. Cut off the shorter wire end. If desired, slide a seed bead or a sterling silver bead onto this wire.

10. To attach to the chain, bend the wire 45° and wrap it around using the round-nose pliers. Slide the loop onto the chain immediately above the 25-mm quartz drop, in the same link where you attached the head pin in steps 7 and 8. Hold the loop with the chain-nose pliers and wrap the wire around to secure. Cut off the excess wire.

11. Attach a total of 10 head pins or twisted wire loop links above the large quartz drop. Use the first four links in the chain as well as the wire loop above the 25-mm quartz drop for attaching these small head pins and wire links (figure 4). To give the gemstone cluster a lush, full effect, attach a detailed head pin or wire link to both sides of these four chain links, as well as the wire loop.

fig. 4

12. After completing one end of the chain, work the other end, repeating steps 5 through 11 to complete the necklace.

13. fig. 5

To wear this necklace, hold both beaded ends in one hand and the loop of the chain in the other hand. Place it around your neck and slip the two beaded ends through the loop in the chain (figure 5).

FANTASTICAL

Have fun making and wearing these splashy earrings, dripping with oodles of bright and colorful beads.

FANTASTICAL

Materials

Approximately 35 apatite rondelles, 3 mm

Approximately 20 pink tourmaline
rondelles, 3 mm

Approximately 20 citrine rondelles, 4 mm

Approximately 22 carnelian rondelles,
4 mm

6 rose quartz rondelles, 5 mm

8 rose quartz briolettes (faceted), 5 mm

8 garnet briolettes (smooth), 4 mm

10 gold-filled beads, 3 mm

16 gold-filled beads, 2 mm

20 gold-filled head pins, 1 inch
(2.5 cm) long

2 gold-filled ball-post earrings with rings

8-inch (20.3 cm) length of 1.5-mm
gold-filled chain

14-inch (35.6 cm) length of 26-gauge
gold-filled wire

Tools

Chain-nose pliers

Round-nose pliers

Wire cutters

Ruler

Techniques

Making Twisted Wire Loop Links
(page 20)

Working with Purchased Earring Findings
(page 24)

Instructions

Make two

1. Cut the chain into two segments of 4 inches (10.2 cm) each.

2. Attach one end of the 26-gauge wire to one of the 4-inch (10.2 cm) chain segments. With the round-nose pliers, grip the wire ¾ inch (1.9 cm) from the end and wrap to make a loop. Place the last link in the chain on the loop. Hold the loop with the chain-nose pliers and twist the wires around to secure. Cut off the shorter wire end.

3. Make a new loop using the remaining wire and the round-nose pliers. Slide the ring of the ball-post earring onto the loop. Hold the wire loop with the chain-nose pliers and wrap the wire around the twist you made in step 2. Cut off the excess wire.

4. Repeat steps 2 and 3 on the opposite end of the chain but attach it to one of the loops in the earring back (figure 1). **fig. 1**

5. Now it's time to simply have fun with oodles of beads! Starting at the front of the earring chain and working toward the back, you'll be attaching extensions on every other link in the chain. The extension will be made with all the different rondelles, briolettes, and round beads, using wire and head pins.

fig. 2

For this design, I chose to make the extensions in the center longer than those at the ends (figure 2), which will hang nearest to your ears, but you can make all the extensions the same length, if desired.

6. To make the head-pin extensions, select a group of two to six stones and beads, reserving the briolettes for step 8. Slide them onto the head pin, bend the head pin 45° and use the round-nose pliers to loop the head pin around.

7. Slide the end of this head pin through a link in the chain until the loop is hanging from it. Hold the loop with the chain-nose pliers and wrap the head pin around to secure. Cut off the excess wire.

8. To make the briolette extensions, use the 26-gauge wire. Slide the wire through a briolette so that ¾ inch (1.9 cm) extends out the other side. Bend the wire up on both sides of the briolette. Make sure the wires fit snugly around the stone, and then twist them together to secure the stone in place. Cut off the shorter wire end.

9. If desired, add a rondelle or a round bead on the wire before looping and attaching it. To do this, make sure the wire is sticking straight up and not pointing to the side. Slide one or two beads or stones of your choice onto the wire.

10. After all your beads are in place, bend the wire 45° and grip it with the round-nose pliers. Loop the wire around. Slide it through one of the links in the chain until the loop is hanging from the link. Hold the loop with the chain-nose pliers and wrap the wire to secure. Cut off the excess wire.

11. Repeat steps 6 through 10 until you've attached extensions along the length of the earring chain.

DANGLE

Display more than a dozen of your favorite large gemstones with a necklace designed to enhance their translucent beauty.

Instructions

Instructions

1. This necklace is casual in its design, with the stones interspersed along the strands, connected by varying lengths of chain. The only technique you really need to know is how to make twisted wire bead links. Select and set aside the largest and/or most beautiful of the tourmaline stones to use in a focal position in step 9.

2. Using the round-nose pliers and the 24-gauge wire, make a loop in the wire about ¾ inch (1.9 cm) from the end. Slide this loop onto the chain. Hold the wire with the chain-nose pliers and twist the wires around to secure. Cut off the shorter wire end.

3. Slide one large tourmaline stone onto the wire. Bend the wire 45°. Hold the wire with the round-nose pliers and loop the wire around to secure.

4. Cut the chain you previously attached, making it between ½ to 2½ inches (1.3 to 5.1 cm) in length.

5. Place the remaining chain onto this loop. Hold the loop with the round-nose pliers and wrap the wire around to secure. Cut off the excess wire.

6. Make a new loop in the wire ¾ inch (1.9 cm) from the end. Run the loop onto the last link in the already-connected chain. Hold this loop and twist the wires around to secure. Cut off the shorter wire end.

7. Slide a variety of smaller beads onto the wire. For example: 4-mm round stone, 2-mm gold-filled bead, 8-mm rondelle, 2-mm gold-filled bead, and 4-mm round stone. Another example: 3-mm rondelle, 8-mm oval bead, and 3-mm rondelle. Feel free to mix and match the small stones in any order you wish in a fashion similar to the examples above, or in another design of your choosing. After you've added the beads, add a new length of chain to each twisted loop link and wrap the loop to secure.

8. Continue placing the large tourmaline stones and the smaller beads and stones on this length of chain until

---

Finished size: 19½ inches (48.3 cm); longest dangle, 4¾ inches (12 cm)

Materials

18 large watermelon tourmaline stones, 12 to 20 mm

9 peridot beads (oval), 8 mm

7 aventurine beads, 4 mm

10 pink tourmaline rondelles, 3 mm

6 chrysoprase rondelles, 8 mm

10 garnet beads, 4 mm

4 gold-filled beads, 2 mm

5 gold-filled beads, 3 mm

5 gold-filled ball-end head pins, 1½ inches (3.8 cm) long

1 gold-filled lobster clasp

48-inch (122 cm) length of 1.5-mm gold-filled chain

2-inch (5.1 cm) length of 2.5-mm gold-filled chain (for the toggle)

60-inch (152.4 cm) length of 24-gauge gold-filled wire

Tools

Chain-nose pliers

Round-nose pliers

Wire cutters

Large rubberized chain-nose pliers

Ruler

Techniques

Making Twisted Wire Loop Links (page 20)

Making Catches and Clasps (page 22)

you've completed 8 inches (20.3 cm). Stretch out this completed strand in front of you and start working on the second 8-inch (20.3 cm) length. You'll need to complete a total of six 8-inch (20.3 cm) strands for the necklace. As you're working on the subsequent strands, be sure to periodically place them next to the completed ones to see how the stones are lining up in relation to each other. Avoid massing the stones in one area, and be sure to alternate the colors.

9. After the six strands are completed, you're ready to place the focal tourmaline stone that you set aside in step 1. Make a new wire loop with the 24-gauge wire. Place the end links of all six strands on this loop. Hold the loop with the round-nose pliers and twist the wires around to secure. Cut off the shorter wire end.

10. fig. 1

Slide the large tourmaline stone onto the wire. Bend the wire 45°. Hold it with the round-nose pliers and loop the wire around, but do not wrap it just yet (figure 1). Set it aside while you work on other parts of the necklace.

11. Repeat steps 2 through 7 to make four more lengths of chain, each about 1½ to 2½ inches (3.8 to 6.4 cm) in length, varying the length slightly for each piece of chain.

12. Finish off each piece of chain. First, place a variety of stones on one head pin. Then bend the head pin 45° and loop it around the round-nose pliers. Slide this loop onto the end link of one of the pieces of chain. Hold the loop with the chain-nose pliers and wrap this wire end around to secure. Cut off the excess wire.

13. Repeat step 12 for all four pieces of chain, varying the stones you use each time.

14. Place all four of the completed pieces of chain on the loop that you set aside in step 10. Then hold the loop using the chain-nose pliers and wrap the wire around to secure. Cut off the excess wire.

15. Moving to the closure of the necklace, attach the clasp to three successive strands that you finished in step 8. First, make a new loop in the wire ¾ inch (1.9 cm) from the end. Place the three strands on the loop. Hold the loop with the round-nose pliers and wrap the wires together. Cut off the shorter wire end.

16. Hold the remaining wire with the round-nose pliers and wrap it around again. Slide the clasp onto this loop. Hold the loop with the chain-nose pliers and wrap the wire around the twist you made in step 15.

17. Now make the catch for the clasp. Make a new loop in the 24-gauge wire. Slide onto this loop the remaining three strands. Twist the wires together to secure. Cut off the shorter wire end.

18. Grip the wire using the rubberized round-nose pliers. Loop the wire around. Hold the loop with the rubberized pliers and wrap the wire around the twist you made in step 17 to secure. Cut off the excess wire.

19. To add a final detail for the back of the necklace, make a drop chain, which can also be used as a toggle. First, make a loop in the 24-gauge wire using the round-nose pliers. Run the wire through the smaller loop of the catch for the clasp to attach the loops to each other. Hold this loop with the chain-nose pliers and twist the wires around to secure. Cut off the shorter wire end.

20. Make a new loop using the round-nose pliers. Place the 2-inch (5.1 cm) length of large-link chain onto this loop. Grab the loop with the chain-nose pliers and wrap the wire around the twist you made in step 19. Cut off the excess wire.

21. Select the remaining head pin and slide on your choice of stones. Bend the wire 45°. Loop this wire around the round-nose pliers and place the loop on the end of the chain. Hold the loop with the chain-nose pliers and wrap the wire around to secure. Cut off the excess wire.

CLEOPATRA

The intriguing qualities of green onyx and chrysoprase are displayed to perfection in this simple yet stylish earring design.

Instructions

Make two

Finished size: 1½ inches (3.8 cm)

Materials

2 green onyx briolettes, 12 mm

2 chrysoprase briolettes, 6 mm

2 gold-filled ball-post earrings
with open rings

12-inch (30.5 cm) length of
24-gauge gold-filled wire

4-inch (10.2 cm) length of
26-gauge gold-filled wire

Tools

Chain-nose pliers

Round-nose pliers

Wire cutters

Large rubberized round-nose pliers

Ruler

Techniques

Making Twisted Wire Loop Links
(page 20)

Working with Purchased Earring
Findings (page 24)

1. With wire cutters, cut the 12-inch (30.5 cm) length of 24-gauge wire into two 6-inch (15.2 cm) segments.

2. Select one of the wires and slide a 12-mm green onyx briolette onto the middle of it. Bend the wires on both sides of the bead until they cross, and then twist them around once to secure the briolette in place.

3. **fig. 1**  Using the large rubberized round-nose pliers, bend both wires into a curve (figure 1). Before continuing, make sure the wires are curved to a pleasing size to accommodate the 6-mm chrysoprase briolette; hold it in the middle of the curve to check. Adjust the size of the curve as necessary.

4. Keeping the wires crossed and using the round-nose pliers, grasp one wire on the inside of the cross and loop it around (figure 2). **fig. 2**

5. With the chain-nose pliers, hold both the loop you've just made and the opposite wire and twist them around just above the loop (figure 3). Cut off one wire above the twist. **fig. 3**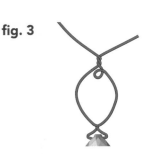

6. Loop the remaining wire around and slide the ring of the ball-post earring onto the wire.

7. Hold this loop with the chain-nose pliers and wrap the wire around the twist you made in step 5. Cut off the excess wire.

8. Cut the 4-inch (10.2 cm) length of 26-gauge wire in half, making two 2-inch (5.1 cm) lengths. Slide a 6-mm chrysoprase briolette onto one wire about ¾ inch (1.9 cm) from the end. Bend both ends up until the wires are crossing.

9. Twist the wires around one and one-half times and cut off the shorter wire end. Adjust the remaining wire so that it is facing forward (not to the side).

10. Using the round-nose pliers, loop this wire and slide it through the bottom loop you created on the earring.

11. After one loop is hanging from the other, use the chain-nose pliers to hold this new loop and wrap the wire around the twist you made in step 9. Cut off the excess wire.

OCEAN
WAVES

Use a jig to make the wire waves, then link them with abalone and lapis lazuli for this bracelet inspired by the sea.

Instructions

1. Use the jig and the 22-gauge wire to make eight wire "waves." Use a three-loop peg spacing as shown in figure 1.

fig. 1

2. To create the waves, wrap the wire around the pegs following the directional pattern shown in figure 2.

fig. 2

Finish   Start

3. **fig. 3**

After creating the wave shape, remove it from the jig. Using the chain-nose pliers, hold one of the side loops. Wrap one end of the wire around to secure the loop in place. Cut off the excess wire. Do the same for the loop on the other side (figure 3). You may need to pull the two ends slightly to make sure the center loop holds its shape. Then use the rubberized round-nose pliers to squeeze and flatten the wave as much as possible. Repeat this for all eight of the waves.

4. Using the round-nose pliers, make a loop in the 24-gauge wire about ¾ inch (1.9 cm) from the end. Slide the clasp onto this loop. Hold the loop with the chain-nose pliers, and then twist the wires around to secure. Cut off the shorter wire end. Slide on a 15-mm rectangular abalone bead and bend the wire 45°. Hold this wire with the round-nose pliers and wrap it around to make a loop.

5. Slide the center loop of a wave onto this wire loop, hold the loop with the chain-nose pliers, and wrap the wire around to secure. Cut off the excess wire.

6. Using the round-nose pliers, make a new loop in the 24-gauge wire about ¾ inch (1.9 cm) from the end. Slide the loop onto one of the side loops of the wave. Grab this loop with the chain-nose pliers and twist the wires together to secure. Cut off the shorter wire end.

Finished size: 7½ inches (19 cm)

Materials

4 abalone beads (rectangular), 15 mm

8 lapis lazuli beads, 6 mm

35-inch (88.9 cm) length of 22-gauge sterling silver wire

33-inch (83.8 cm) length of 24-gauge sterling silver wire

1 sterling silver figure-eight lobster clasp

Tools

Jig

Round-nose pliers

Chain-nose pliers

Large rubberized round-nose pliers

Wire cutters

Techniques

Making Twisted Wire Loop Links (page 20)

Using Special Tools (jigs, page 25)

7. Place a 6-mm lapis lazuli bead onto the wire, bend the wire 45° and loop it around again. Slide this loop onto the side loop of another wire wave and wrap it closed using the chain-nose pliers. Cut off the excess wire.

8. Repeat steps 6 and 7 on the other side loop of the wave, ending up with two 6-mm lapis lazuli beads across from each other on the bracelet.

9. Repeat steps 4 through 8 three times to add the remaining wire waves and stones, sliding the wire through the center loop of the wave instead of through the clasp in step 4. Make sure the final wave is attached with its center loop facing out, as this loop will serve as a catch for the clasp. (Don't add another clasp here as described in step 4, because the wire loop will do just fine as a catch.)

SPOTLIGHT

A large blue topaz is the focal point for this stunning necklace, with seed beads adding artistic detail.

Finished size: 16¼ inches (41.3 cm);
focal element, 2 ⅞ inches (7.3 cm)

Materials

1 large blue topaz, 40 mm

6 blue topaz briolettes, 10 mm

5 light blue chalcedony briolettes, 10 mm

4 blue topaz beads, 3 mm

1 gold-filled bead, 3 mm

Brown seed beads

6 to 8 gold-filled ball-end head pins,
1½ inches (3.8 cm) long

1 gold-filled ball-end head pin, 2 inches
(5.1 cm) long

1 gold-filled hook-and-eye clasp

15-inch (38.1 cm) length of 4-mm gold-filled
krinkle chain

24-inch (61 cm) length of 24-gauge gold-filled wire

8-inch (20.3 cm) length of 22-gauge gold-filled wire

Tools

Chain-nose pliers

Round-nose pliers

Wire cutters

Large rubberized round-nose pliers

Ruler

Techniques

Making Twisted Wire Loop Links (page 20)

Making Catches and Clasps (page 22)

Working with Head Pins (page 23)

Instructions

1. Cut the gold-filled krinkle chain into three 1-inch (2.5 cm) segments and one 12-inch (30.5 cm) segment. Before cutting short chain segments, I always count the links to make certain that the segments are exactly the same length.

2. Using the round-nose pliers, make a loop in the 24-gauge wire about ¾ inch (1.9 cm) from the end. Take one of the 1-inch (2.5 cm) chain segments and place an end link onto the loop. Hold the loop with the chain-nose pliers and twist the wires together. Cut off the shorter wire end.

3. Holding the loop with the chain-nose pliers, bend the wire about 45°. Make a new loop with the round-nose pliers.

4. **fig. 1**

Select the 12-inch (30.5 cm) chain segment and fold it in half to locate the center link in the chain. Attach the loop made in step 3 to this center link. Hold the loop with the chain-nose pliers and wrap the wire around the twist you made in step 2 (figure 1). Cut off the excess wire.

5. Select the 2-inch (5.1 cm) head pin and slide the 3-mm gold-filled bead onto it, followed by the large 40-mm topaz. Bend the wire of the head pin 45°, and wrap it around the round-nose pliers.

6. Attach the head pin loop to the end of the 1-inch (2.5 cm) chain. Hold the loop with the chain-nose pliers and wrap the wire to secure. Cut off the excess wire.

7. Select ten 10-mm briolettes (five each of blue topaz and light blue chalcedony) and attach them along the 1-inch (2.5 cm) chain with the 24-gauge wire. Use the following method: Slide ¾ inch (1.9 cm) of the wire through each briolette and bend up both wire ends until they cross. Twist the wires together to secure. Cut off the shorter wire end. Bend the longer wire 45°, and wrap it around the round-nose pliers. Slide the wire through one of the links in the 1-inch (2.5. cm) chain. Hold the loop with the chain-nose pliers and wrap the wire around the first twist in the wire. Evenly space the 10 briolettes throughout the 1-inch (2.5. cm) chain.

8. **fig. 2**   **fig. 3**

Twirl six to eight head pins using the following technique. Wrap the pin around one jaw of the round-nose pliers by taking hold of the ball-end of the pin and twirling it around (figure 2). To continue the twist, release the pliers, rotate the pin slightly, grab on with the pliers again, and twist. Because the pliers are tapered, you'll need to be careful not to taper your twist. So to keep it even, flip the head pin when it is halfway done and continue wrapping it around the jaw. Leave a straight length of ¾ inch (1.9 cm) at the end (figure 3).

9. Select the brown seed beads and slide them onto a twirled head pin, stopping when you reach the straight part of the pin. Repeat for all of the head pins.

10. Attach the bead-covered head pins to the 1-inch (2.5 cm) section of chain, intermixing the head pins among the briolettes. Using the round-nose pliers, hold the straight end of each head pin and wrap it around to form a loop. Attach this loop to one of the chain links between two briolettes. Hold the loop with the chain-nose pliers and wrap the wire around to secure. Cut off the excess wire. Repeat this step to attach all of the head pins, forming a cluster around the large topaz.

11. Begin working on the closure of the necklace. To add interest and detail, you'll be removing some of the chain length and replacing it with beaded wire in the steps that follow.

12. Using the round-nose pliers, make a loop in the 22-gauge wire by holding the wire about ¾ inch (1.9 cm) from the end and wrapping it around. Attach this loop to one of the 12-inch (30.5 cm) chain ends. Hold the loop with the chain-nose pliers and twist to secure. Cut off the shorter wire end.

13. Slide 1½ inches (3.8 cm) of seed beads and two 3-mm topaz beads onto the wire. Bend the wire 45°, and again wrap it around the round-nose pliers. Slide a clasp onto this loop, then hold the loop with the chain-nose pliers and wrap the wire around to secure. Cut off the excess wire.

14. Bend the beaded wire ever so slightly to conform to the curve of the neck.

15. Repeat steps 12 through 14 on the other end of the 12-inch (30.5 cm) chain, this time placing a 1-inch (2.5 cm) length of chain onto the loop in step 13, instead of a clasp.

16. If you choose, you can make a clasp from wire instead of using a purchased one. To make a clasp, begin with the 22-gauge wire and the round-nose pliers, making a loop in the wire about ¾ inch (1.9 cm) from the end. Attach the loop to the end of the 1½-inch (3.8 cm) beaded wire end. Hold this loop with the chain-nose pliers and wrap the wire around to secure. Cut off the excess wire.

17. fig. 4

With the rubberized round-nose pliers, wrap around the wire to form a loop. Put the round-nose pliers around the wire at the same level as the wrapped wire section, and then loop the wire around (figure 4). Cut off the excess wire.

18. Make the catch by forming a new loop in the 22-gauge wire. Slide this loop through the wire loop at the end of the beaded wire. Twist the wires together to secure. Cut off the shorter wire end.

19. Grip the wire with the rubberized round-nose pliers and wrap the wire around. Hold the loop with these same pliers and wrap the wire around the twist you made in step 18 to secure. Cut off the excess wire.

20. For a final detail on the toggle chain, make a loop in the 22-gauge wire using the round-nose pliers. Slide the wire through the smaller loop of the catch to attach the loops to each other. Hold this loop with the chain-nose pliers and twist the wires around to secure. Cut off the shorter wire end.

21. Make a new loop using the round-nose pliers and place the remaining 1-inch (2.5 cm) length of chain onto this loop. Grip the loop with the chain-nose pliers and wrap the wire around the twist you made in step 20 to secure. Cut off the excess wire.

22. Slide the 24-gauge wire through the one remaining blue topaz 10-mm briolette so that ¾ inch (1.9 cm) extends from one end. Bend both ends upward until they cross. Twist the wires together and cut off the shorter wire end.

23. Make a loop with the round-nose pliers and string it through the end of the chain. Hold the loop with the chain-nose pliers and wrap the wire around the twisted part to secure. Cut off the excess wire. This chain section can play the part of a back detail as well as a toggle to extend the length of the necklace.

SNOW

Combine a flurry of pearls with sterling silver hammered disks and hoops to make a free-flowing necklace with ever-changing shapes and textures.

SNOW

Finished size: 17½ inches (44.5 cm)

Materials

34 pearls (disks), some 10 mm and some 12 mm

14 sterling silver hammered disks, 12 mm

13 sterling silver hammered hoops, 15 mm

1 sterling silver lobster clasp

80-inch (203.2 cm) length of 2.5-mm sterling silver chain

160-inch (406.4 cm) length of sterling silver 24-gauge wire

4-inch (12.7 cm) length of sterling silver 22-gauge wire

Tools

Chain-nose pliers

Round-nose pliers

Wire cutters

Large rubberized round-nose pliers

Ruler

Techniques

Making Twisted Wire Loop Links (page 20)

Making Catches and Clasps (page 22)

Instructions

1. Cut the chain into ½-inch (1.3 cm) and 1½-inch (3.8 cm) segments.

2. Using the round-nose pliers, make a loop in the 24-gauge wire about ¾ inch (1.9 cm) from the end. Slide this loop onto the chain. Hold the wire with the chain-nose pliers and twist the wires around to secure. Cut off the shorter wire end.

3. Slide one 10- or 12-mm pearl onto the wire. Bend the wire 45°. Hold the wire with the round-nose pliers and loop the wire around.

4. Now slide a new chain end onto this loop. Hold the loop with the round-nose pliers and wrap the wire around to secure. Cut off the excess wire.

5. Select a sterling silver hoop. Slide the 24-gauge wire through the hoop. Bend the wire so that it surrounds the hoop tightly and bend it again so that the wires cross; twist the wire ends together and cut off the shorter wire end. Using the round-nose pliers, loop the wire around and slide it through the final link in the chain.

6. Hold the wire loop with the chain-nose pliers and wrap the wire around the twist you made in step 5 to secure (figure 1). Cut off the excess wire.

fig. 1

7. Attach a new piece of chain onto the opposite side of the hoop, using the same twisted wire loop link technique from steps 5 and 6.

8. Make a new loop in the wire about ¾ inch (1.9 cm) from the end and place it onto the end of the new piece of chain. Hold this loop with the chain-nose pliers and twist the wires around to secure. Cut off the shorter wire end. This time, slide on perhaps one 10-mm disk pearl, one 12-mm disk pearl, and one 10-mm disk pearl. Bend the wire 45°, and loop it around using the round-nose pliers. Place it onto a new piece of chain. Hold the loop with the chain-nose pliers. Wrap the wire around to secure and cut off the excess.

9. Select one of the silver disks and slide the wire through one of its holes. Bend the wire until both ends are crossed tightly. Twist the wires together and cut off the shorter wire end. Wrap the wire around using the round-nose pliers and slide it through the final link in the chain. Hold the loop with the chain-nose pliers and wrap the wire around the twist you just made to secure (figure 2). Cut off the excess wire.

fig. 2

10. Attach another wire loop, as in step 9, to the other side of this silver disk and follow with another piece of chain.

11. Continue adding on segments as described above in steps 2 through 10, connecting them with twisted wire loop links. The chain segments should alternate between ½ inch (1.3 cm) and 1½ inches (3.8 cm). Switch from pearls to silver hoop or disks as you go along. Feel free to use one, two, or three pearls at a time, depending on your preference.

12. As the strand reaches 14 inches (35.6 cm) in length, end the strand with a piece of chain. Set it aside and begin a new strand. Make a total of five 14-inch (35.6 cm) strands, each beginning and ending with a piece of chain.

13. After completing all five strands, join them onto a single loop. Using the round-nose pliers, hold the 22-gauge wire about ¾ inch (1.9 cm) from the end and loop the wire around. Place the end links of all five strands onto this loop. Hold the loop with the chain-nose pliers and twist the wire around to secure. Cut off the shorter wire end.

14. Using the round-nose pliers, make a new loop in the wire and slide the clasp onto this loop. Hold the

loop with the chain-nose pliers and wrap the wire around the twist you made in step 13. Cut off the excess wire.

15. Using the round-nose pliers, make a new loop in the 22-gauge wire and slide the opposite end links of the five strands onto this loop. (Before placing the strands onto the loop, let them all hang down to make sure they are not tangled or twisted.)

16. After all five strands are on the loop, hold this loop with the chain-nose pliers and twist the wires around to secure. Cut off the shorter wire end.

17. Using the rubberized round-nose pliers, wrap the wire around to make a large loop. Grip this loop with the rubberized pliers and wrap the wire around the twist you made in step 16. Cut off the excess wire.

WEEPING WILLOW

Add a natural touch to your wardrobe with these earthy earrings, accented with a touch of extra looping detail.

Instructions

Finished size: 2¾ inches (7 cm)

Materials

2 copper-colored pearls (disks), 10 mm

18 peridot beads, 4 mm

4 copper-colored pearls, 3 mm

6 green grossular garnet briolettes, 6 mm

4 gold-filled beads, 3 mm

6 gold-filled ball-end head pins, 1 inch (2.5 cm) long

2 gold-filled ball-end head pins, 1½ inches (3.8 cm) long

8-inch (20.3 cm) length of 1.5-mm gold-filled chain

24-inch (61 cm) length of 26-gauge gold-filled wire

Tools

Chain-nose pliers

Round-nose pliers

Wire cutters

Large rubberized round-nose pliers

Ruler

Techniques

Making Twisted Wire Loop Links (page 20)

Making Earring Loops (page 24)

Make two

1. fig. 1

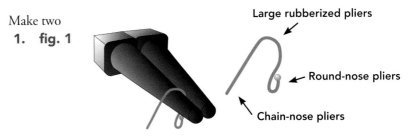

Large rubberized pliers

Round-nose pliers

Chain-nose pliers

Make the earring loops using the 1½-inch (3.8 cm) ball-end head pins. Place the round-nose pliers around the end with the ball. Loop the head pin around until the ball is touching the wire. Use the rubberized round-nose pliers to grip the wire above the loop just created. Bend the wire around the pliers (figure 1). Using the chain-nose pliers, slightly bend up the tip of the wire end for a finishing touch.

2. Cut the chain into two segments of 4 inches (10.2 cm) each. Then cut each of these two 4-inch (10.2 cm) segments into six smaller segments with the following lengths: 1¼ inches (3.2 cm), 1 inch (2.5 cm), 1 inch (2.5 cm), ½ inch (1.3 cm), ⅛ inch (3 mm), and ⅛ inch (3 mm). Keep these lengths of chain separate, being careful not to mix them. Each group of six segments will be used to make one earring.

3. Using the 26-gauge wire, make a loop about ½ inch (1.3 cm) from the end. Slide this loop onto the earring. Grab the loop with the chain-nose pliers and wrap the wire around to secure.

4. Place one 10-mm copper-colored pearl onto this wire and bend the wire 45°. Using the round-nose pliers, loop it around. Place onto this loop one group of the six chain segments cut in step 2. Hold the loop with the chain-nose pliers and twist the wires around to secure. Cut off the shorter wire end. To add extra looping detail, continue looping the wire around and around until you have your desired look. Cut off the remaining wire. *Note:* If the end of the wire sticks out a little after you've cut off the excess, use the chain-nose pliers to push the wire end closer to the wrapped wire.

5. Now that you have all of the major parts in place, add the details. For this design, I attached briolettes and beads using wire loop links and ball-end head pins; feel free to add more, fewer, and even a different set of stones. The briolettes are attached to the bottom links of three different pieces of chain. To attach them, first run the 26-gauge wire through the briolette with ¾ inch (1.9 cm) extending out the other end. Bend both wire ends up until they cross. Twist them around to secure the briolette. Cut off the shorter wire end.

6. **fig. 2**

Using the round-nose pliers, loop the wire around. Slide this loop onto the bottom link in the selected chain. Hold the loop with the chain-nose pliers and wrap the wire around. To add extra looping detail, continue wrapping the wire around until you have your desired look (figure 2). Cut off the excess wire.

7. For the other three pieces of chain, attach head pins with a mixture of beads. For example, I used the following combinations: one peridot bead, one pearl, and one peridot bead; one peridot bead, one pearl, and one gold-filled bead; and one peridot bead and one gold-filled bead. Mix and match the beads to create combinations of stones and colors that you like; there is no right or wrong way.

8. After you've selected what you want to use on the head pin, bend it 45°. Loop it around the round-nose pliers and slide it through the bottom link in the selected chain. Hold this loop with the chain-nose pliers and wrap the wire around. Again, feel free to use the extra looping detail here by continuing to loop the wire around a few more times. Cut off the excess wire.

9. For one final detail, attach a few more 4-mm peridot beads to the middle links of some of the pieces of chain. Again, slide the wire through the bead so you have ¾ inch (1.9 cm) extending out the other end. Bend up both wires and twist them around to secure the bead. Cut off the shorter wire end.

10. Using the round-nose pliers, loop the wire around and place this loop on the middle of one of the pieces of chain. Hold this loop with the chain-nose pliers and wrap the wire around. Cut off the excess wire.

HARMONY

Classy smoky quartz nuggets combine with artistically draped chains to make this lovely pair of earrings.

Finished size: 4⅛ inches (10.5 cm)

Materials

2 smoky quartz nuggets, 20 mm

2 smoky quartz briolettes, 5 mm

36-inch (91.4 cm) length of 1.5-mm gold or gold-filled chain

8-inch (20.3 cm) length of 22-gauge gold-filled wire

4-inch (10.2 cm) length of 26-gauge gold-filled wire

Tools

Chain-nose pliers

Round-nose pliers

Wire cutters

Large rubberized round-nose pliers

Ruler

Techniques

Making Basic Loop Links (page 22)

Making Earring Loops (page 24)

Instructions

Make two

1. Cut the 36-inch (91.4 cm) length of chain into segments. Cut two pieces in each of the following lengths: 2 inches (5.1 cm), 2½ inches (6.4 cm), 3½ inches (8.9 cm), 4½ inches (11.4 cm), and 5½ inches (14 cm). Keep all five sets paired up so you can easily identify the various lengths. *Note:* Before cutting the 2-inch (5.1 cm) chain segments, count the links to make sure you have an odd number. You'll be hanging the earring from the middle link of this chain, which means you need to have an even number of links on either side.

2. **fig. 1**   **fig. 2**

Make a basic loop link using the 22-gauge wire and round-nose pliers. Wrap the very end of the wire around the jaw of the round-nose pliers. After making a nearly full loop (figure 1), rotate the pliers so the outside jaw touches the long end of the wire. Clamp down and bend the wire about 45° to center the loop (figure 2). Be sure to keep the loop open a bit, because you'll need to slide on the chain.

3. Select a 20-mm nugget and slide it onto this wire. Bend the wire and repeat the loop from step 2 to match the other side. Clamp the round-nose pliers on the wire as close to the stone as you can get. Wrap the wire around the pliers until you've made a circle. Nudge in the wire cutters to cut off the excess wire, being careful not to cut too much. You now have the foundation, or focal bead, for making the earring.

Designer's Tip

This bears repeating: When you're matching lengths of chain, count the links to make sure that each pair or set has exactly the same number of links. This way you'll be certain that they are identical and that both earrings match. A difference of even one tiny link can affect the final appearance of your piece of jewelry.

4. fig. 3

Keeping the spaces in the wire loops facing up (figure 3), place one set of chain segments onto one loop, starting with the 2½-inch (6.4 cm), followed by the 3½-inch (8.9 cm), the 4½-inch (11.4 cm), the 5½-inch (14 cm), and finally the 2-inch (5.1 cm) chain. To place a chain, hold the last link on the chain with the chain-nose pliers and slip it onto one wire loop. Making sure the chain doesn't twist,

fig. 4

grab hold of the opposite end of the chain segment you're working with and slide it onto the second loop (figure 4).

5. Repeat step 4 with the remaining four chains.

6. After all the chains are in place, use the round-nose pliers to close the two wire loops. Set aside this part of the earring.

7. Make a wire loop link for one briolette. Using the 24-gauge wire, slide it through the briolette with ¾ inch (1.9 cm) extending out the other side. Bend the wire up on both sides of the stone. Cross the wires so they fit snugly around the top of the stone and, using either your fingers or the chain-nose pliers, twist the wires around. Cut off the shorter wire end.

8. fig. 5

Bend the longer wire 45° just above the twist. Using the round-nose pliers, make a loop. Hold the loop with the chain-nose pliers and wrap the wire back around the twist. Cut off the excess wire (figure 5). Set aside this part of the earring.

9. Finally, make the earring loop and bring it all together. Using the 22-gauge wire and the round-nose pliers, wrap the wire to create a loop with a short end about ½ inch (1.3 cm) long.

10. First, slide onto this loop the briolette, followed by the middle link in the 2-inch (5.1 cm) chain. Slide the two end links of this chain to the top of the wire loops beside the focal bead.

11. After everything is in place, hold the loop with the chain-nose pliers and twist the wire around to secure it. Cut off the shorter wire end.

12. Place the rubberized round-nose pliers at the base of this wire twist and wrap the wire around to shape it into an earring loop. Cut the wire to the desired length.

13. Using the chain-nose pliers, hold the tip of the just-curved earring loop and bend it slightly upward to create a finishing detail (page 24).

KOKOPELLI

Use a jig to make delicate loops in sterling silver wire for a swaying pair of turquoise earrings.

KOKOPELLI

Finished size: 4⅜ inches (12.3 cm)

Materials

2 turquoise briolettes, 10 mm

8 turquoise briolettes, 8 mm

8 labradorite beads, 3 mm

15-inch (38.1 cm) length of 22-gauge sterling silver wire

18-inch (45.7 cm) length of 26-gauge sterling silver wire

Tools

Jig

Chain-nose pliers

Round-nose pliers

Wire cutters

Large rubberized round-nose pliers or nylon-jaw pliers

Ruler

Techniques

Making Earring Loops (page 24)

Using Special Tools (jig, page 25)

Instructions

Make two

1. Cut the 22-gauge wire into segments as follows: two 2½-inch (6.4 cm) segments and two 5-inch (12.7 cm) segments.

2. **fig. 1**

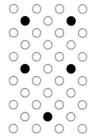

Place the pegs on the jig as shown in figure 1.

3. **fig. 2**

Select one 5-inch (12.7 cm) wire segment and wrap it around the pegs, following the pattern shown in figure 2; leaving an end on the wire about 2½ inches (6.4 cm) long, place the wire against the first peg on the jig. Wrap the wire around the peg, and then follow the pattern around, ending when the wire crosses the other end at the top of the pattern.

4. Carefully remove the wire shape from the jig.

5. Using the chain-nose pliers, grip both wires about 1¼ inches (3.2 cm) above the top loops.

6. fig. 3

Bend the shorter wire 90° to cross the other wire (figure 3).

7. Keeping the chain-nose pliers in place, wrap the bent wire around the straight wire two times. Cut off the excess from this wrapped wire.

8. Place one 3-mm bead on the straight wire and bend the wire above the bead 45°. Make a loop in this wire using the round-nose pliers.

9. Hold this loop with the chain-nose pliers and wrap the wire around to secure.

10. Smooth out the wrapped-wire shape using the rubberized round-nose pliers, or the nylon-jaw pliers, to clamp and flatten the loops between the pliers' jaws. Repeat this process until you've flattened all of the wire shape.

11. Slide the 26-gauge wire through one 10-mm briolette, letting ¾ inch (1.9 cm) extend out the other end. Bend up both wires until they cross tightly. Twist them around each other one full turn. Cut off the shorter wire end.

12. Keep the remaining wire extending straight up from the briolette and slide one 3-mm bead onto it. Bend back the wire and wrap it around the round-nose pliers to form a loop.

13. Slide this loop onto the bottom loop in the wrapped-wire shape. Using the chain-nose pliers, hold this loop and wrap the wire around to secure. Cut off the excess wire.

14. Repeat steps 11 through 13 for the bottom two loops of the wrapped-wire shape, and then again for the two top ones, with the difference of deleting the 3-mm beads for the two top loops. Use the 8-mm briolettes for all four of these.

15. To make an earring loop, select one of the 2½-inch (6.4 cm) segments of the 22-gauge wire. Use the round-nose pliers to grip the wire ¾ inch (1.9 cm) from the end. Wrap the wire around the pliers to form a loop. Slide this loop through the top loop of the wire shape.

16. Grip the loop with the chain-nose pliers and twist the two wire ends around each other. Cut off the shorter wire end.

17. Using the rubberized round-nose pliers, hold the wire just above the twist and wrap the wire around one jaw of the pliers to create the rounded shape of an earring loop. Cut the wire to the length you desire. Use these same pliers, or the nylon-jaw pliers, to squeeze the whole earring shape to flatten and straighten it.

18. I also like to add a little flip at the end of the wire as a finishing detail. To create this effect, use the round-nose pliers to grip the tip of the wire and bend it up very slightly (page 24).

ABACUS

This fascinating necklace is interesting to make and wear, quietly reminding all who see it of the importance of balance.

Finished size: 20 inches (50.8 cm); longest dangle, 2 inches (5.1 cm)

Materials

3 garnet briolettes, 6 mm

1 garnet round disk bead, 4 mm

2 garnet round bead, 5 mm

4 garnet rondelles, 3 mm

1 garnet drop, 5 mm

2 citrine rectangle beads, 8 mm

3 irregular gold beads, 6 mm

2 irregular gold beads, 4 mm

1 seven-hole gold-filled sterling silver separator bar, or 2 four-hole sterling silver separator bars

10 gold-filled ball-end head pins, 1 inch (2.5 cm) long

1 gold-filled lobster clasp

24-inch (61 cm) length of 1.5-mm gold-filled chain

2½-inch (6.4 cm) length of 3.5-mm gold-filled chain (for toggle)

12-inch (30.5 cm) length of 26-gauge gold-filled wire

6-inch (15.2 cm) length of 24-gauge gold-filled wire

Tools

Chain-nose pliers

Round-nose pliers

Wire cutters

Ruler

Glue

Techniques

Making Twisted Wire Loop Links (page 20)

Making Catches and Clasps (page 22)

Instructions

1. fig. 1

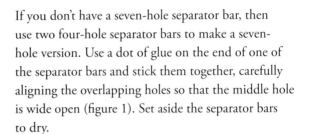

If you don't have a seven-hole separator bar, then use two four-hole separator bars to make a seven-hole version. Use a dot of glue on the end of one of the separator bars and stick them together, carefully aligning the overlapping holes so that the middle hole is wide open (figure 1). Set aside the separator bars to dry.

2. With wire cutters, cut off a 16-inch (40.6 cm) segment from the 24-inch (61 cm) length of 1.5-mm chain. Using the round-nose pliers and 24-gauge wire, make a loop in the wire about ¾ inch (1.9 cm) from the end. Slide it onto the end link of the chain. Use the chain-nose pliers to hold this loop and twist the wires around to secure. Cut off the shorter wire end.

3. Make a new loop in this wire and slide on the lobster clasp. Hold this loop with the chain-nose pliers and wrap the wire around the twist you made in step 2. Cut off the excess wire.

4. Using the round-nose pliers again, make a new wire loop. Slide it onto the opposite end of the chain. Hold it with the chain-nose pliers and twist it around to secure. Cut off the shorter wire end.

Designer's Tips

As a reminder, make sure that the chain you select for the toggle has links large enough to accommodate the lobster clasp.

For this necklace, you'll want to have all stones on the separator bar in balance so the necklace hangs nicely. Use your judgment about whether to add or subtract stones, and where to place them on the separator bar.

8. Make a new loop in the 26-gauge wire using the round-nose pliers. Slide the ¼-inch (6 mm) chain segment onto the loop. Hold the loop and twist the wires to secure. Cut off the shorter wire end.

9. Take the seven-hole separator bar (or the two firmly glued separator bars) and slide the wire through the middle hole. (If you're using the combined separator bar, this middle hole is where the two bars overlap, forming a single hole.)

10. Carefully bend this wire 45° and make a new loop. Place a 1-inch (2.5 cm) segment of chain on this loop. Hold the loop with the chain-nose pliers and wrap the wire around to secure.

11. From this point on, use the remaining instructions as a guide for constructing the necklace. The goal is to have all elements on the separator bar evenly in balance when you're wearing the necklace. Use your judgment about whether to add or subtract stones, which will depend on their weight.

5. Loop this wire again and slide on the 2½-inch (5.1 cm) toggle chain. Hold the loop with the chain-nose pliers and wrap the wire around the twist you made in step 4. Cut off the excess wire.

6. Using the round-nose pliers, make a loop in the 26-gauge wire ¾ inch (1.9 cm) from the end. Locate the middle link in the 16-inch (40.6 cm) necklace chain and slide this loop through it. Use the chain-nose pliers to twist the wires together. Cut off the shorter wire end.

7. Slide one 8-mm citrine rectangle bead onto the wire and bend the wire 45°. Grip the wire with the round-nose pliers and wrap the wire around. Place a ¼-inch (6 mm) segment of chain onto this loop and close the loop by holding it with the chain-nose pliers and wrapping the wire around to secure. Cut off the excess wire.

12. Make a loop in the 26-gauge wire using the round-nose pliers. Slide the loop through the bottom link of the chain, holding it with the chain-nose pliers, and wrap the wires around to secure. Cut off the shorter wire end. Slide on a 5-mm round bead.

13. Bend the wire 45° and loop it around the round-nose pliers. Place a ¼-inch (6 mm) piece of chain on the loop. Hold the loop with the chain-nose pliers and wrap the wire around to secure. Cut off the excess wire.

14. Select one of the head pins. Slide on one 6-mm gold bead and one 3-mm rondelle. Bend the head pin 45° and loop it around with the chain-nose pliers. Slide it through the final link in the ¼-inch (6 mm) chain you attached in step 13. Hold the loop with the chain-nose pliers and wrap around to secure. Cut off the excess wire.

15. fig. 2

For the six remaining holes in the separator bar, attach the pieces of chain with head pins. Holding one head pin, bend it 45° right at the top. Then place it through one hole (figure 2). Hold the head

fig. 3

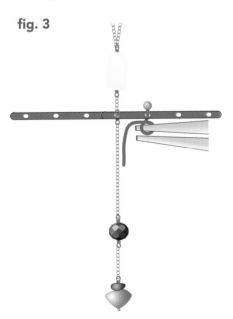

pin with the round-nose pliers, as close as possible to the separator bar, and loop the wire of the head pin around (figure 3).

16. After making the loop, slide on the chain segment. Hold this loop with the chain-nose pliers and wrap the wire around to secure.

17. fig. 4

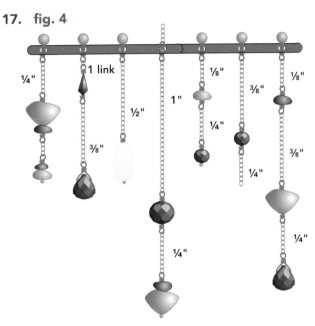

To make a balanced separator-bar design similar to the one shown, use the pattern shown in figure 4 as a guide for chain measurements and bead placement, using twisted wire loop links to attach the segments. Complete the holes from the middle to the outside. Be sure to try on the necklace while you're working on it so you can see how the pieces balance, and make adjustments as necessary, keeping in mind that longer does not mean heavier. Several stones on a short chain will often outweigh a longer chain with fewer stones.

18. After finishing the front piece of the necklace, work on the toggle in the back, adding one final detail. Select a head pin, slide on a few stones, bend the wire 45°, and loop it around the round-nose pliers. Slide the loop onto the end of the toggle chain. Hold the loop with the chain-nose pliers and wrap the wire around to secure. Cut off the excess wire.

Finished size: 1¾ inches (4.4 cm)

Materials

12 malachite beads, 6 mm

12 malachite beads, 4 mm

28 apatite rondelles, 3 mm

2 gold-filled ear clips with ball and ring

8 gold-filled head pins, ½ inches (3.8 cm) long

12-inch (30.5 cm) length of 22-gauge gold-filled wire

Tools

Chain-nose pliers

Round-nose pliers

Wire cutters

Large rubberized round-nose pliers

Ruler

Techniques

Making Twisted Wire Loop Links (page 20)

Working with Purchased Earring Findings (page 24)

Designer's Tip

I used purchased ear clips for this pair of earrings, an option you may prefer. However, you can easily substitute other prefabricated findings, such as ball-post earrings, lever-back earrings, traditional French ear wires, and more.

Instructions

Make two

1. Cut the 12-inch (30.5 cm) length of wire to make two 6-inch (15.6 cm) lengths.

2. **fig. 1**

Using the round-nose pliers, grip the center of one 6-inch (15.6 cm) wire segment and make a loop. Slide this loop onto the ring on one of the ear clips. After the wire loop is hanging from the ring on the ear clip, hold the wire loop with the chain-nose pliers and twist the two wires together two times (figure 1).

3. Place one 3-mm rondelle, one 6-mm round bead, and one 3-mm rondelle on one end of the wire. Using the round-nose pliers, grip the end of this wire and make a loop.

4.

fig. 2

After the wire is completely looped around one time, use either the chain-nose pliers or the rubberized chain-nose pliers to hold the loop between its jaws. Start rotating the pliers to continue the spiral (figure 2). *Note:* If you are not using the rubberized pliers, be very careful when you are clamping down, because you can easily put unattractive dents in the wire.

IVY

Shiny malachite beads capture the essence of all things green in this pair of stylish clip earrings.

5. Continue the spiral until the three beads are snug but with enough remaining space to add two head pins.

6. Repeat steps 3 through 5 on the other end of the wire.

7. Select one of the head pins and slide on these beads in the following order: one 3-mm rondelle, one 4-mm round bead, one 3-mm rondelle, one 6-mm round bead, one 3-mm rondelle, one 4-mm round bead, and one 3-mm rondelle.

8. fig. 3

Bend the head pin 45° and use the round-nose pliers to loop it around. Slide the loop onto the earring segment, between the first rondelle and the 6-mm round bead (figure 3).

9. After the head pin is in place, grip the loop with the chain-nose pliers and wrap the wire around to secure. Cut off the excess wire.

10. Repeat steps 8 and 9 on the other side.

11. Select another head pin and slide on these beads in the following order: one 4-mm round bead, one 6-mm round bead, and one 3-mm rondelle. Bend the wire 45° and loop it around using the round-nose pliers.

12. fig. 4

Slide this loop onto the end of the earring segment, between the final rondelle and the spiraled wire (figure 4).

13. Grip this loop with the chain-nose pliers and wrap the wire around to secure. Cut off the excess wire.

14. Repeat steps 11 through 13 on the other side to finish the earring.

STARBURST

A fabulous cluster of quartz and hematite
stones is the focus of this exceptional bracelet.

Finished size: 8¾ inches (22.2 cm)

Materials

7 hematite beads (faceted), 6 mm

14 hematite beads (faceted), 4 mm

12 hematite rondelles (faceted), 5 mm

12 rose quartz rondelles (faceted), 5 mm

14 cherry quartz beads (faceted), 4 mm

22 sterling silver beads, 3 mm

27 sterling silver ball-end head pins, 1 inch (2.5 cm) long

2 three-strand end bars

1 sterling silver figure-eight lobster clasp

36-inch (91.4 cm) length of 1.5-mm sterling silver chain

1-inch (2.5 cm) length of 2.5-mm sterling silver chain (for the toggle)

10-inch (25.4 cm) length of 22-gauge sterling silver wire

14-inch (35.6 cm) length of 24-gauge sterling silver wire

Tools

Jig with large ¼-inch (6 mm) pegs

Chain-nose pliers

Round-nose pliers

Wire cutters

Large rubberized round-nose pliers

Ruler

Tape (optional)

Techniques

Making Twisted Wire Loop Links (page 20)

Working with Head Pins (page 23)

Using Special Tools (jigs, page 25)

Instructions

1. To make this bracelet, start from the center and work your way out. To begin, cut the chain into twelve 3-inch (7.6 cm) segments. It's very important for this project that each of the 12 chain segments has exactly the same number of links. I highly recommend measuring only the first segment, then counting the links for the other 11 before cutting them to make sure all the segments are identical.

2. **fig. 1**
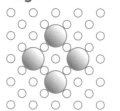
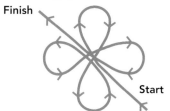
fig. 2

Place the ¼-inch (6 mm) pegs on the jig as shown in figure 1. Wrap the 22-gauge wire in a four-leaf-clover pattern, following the directional pattern shown in figure 2. Carefully remove the wire shape from the jig. Use the rubberized round-nose pliers to squeeze and flatten the wire shape as much as possible.

3. Very carefully twist the top and bottom clover leaves 180° to secure the loops into place while holding onto the rest of the clover shape with the full jaws of the chain-nose pliers.

4. Slide six of the 3-inch (7.6 cm) chain segments onto the two open loops. (This length of chain may seem very short; however, the bracelet needs to fit snugly on the wrist. Therefore, I recommend keeping

Designer's Tip

I recommend that you practice making this clover a few times with inexpensive wire to make sure you've mastered the technique. Then make it with sterling silver or gold-filled wire for the jewelry piece.

the chain this length. If it turns out to be too tight, add length to the bracelet while working steps 7 through 9.)

5.

fig. 3

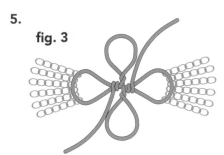

Wrap each wire end around the base of the opposite leaf (figure 3). Cut off the excess wire. Congratulations—you've completed the hardest part!

6. Cut off one link at the end of each of the two middle chains (the third and fourth ones) on both sides of the clover shape. If the chain is very thin, you might need to cut off two links. This adjustment will help all the chains fall evenly on the bracelet after you attach the clasp.

7. Using the round-nose pliers, make a loop in the 24-gauge wire about ¾ inch (1.9 cm) from the end. Slide chains 1 and 2 on one side onto this loop. Hold the loop with the chain-nose pliers and twist the wires around to secure. Cut off the shorter wire.

8. Place one 4-mm bead followed by one 3-mm silver bead onto the wire, bend it 45°, make a new loop with the round-nose pliers, and slide this loop through one of the side loops of an end bar. Repeat this step two more times, first with the third and fourth chains, and then with the fifth and sixth chains, connecting them to the other loops on the end bar. You'll now have all six of the chains connected in pairs to the beads, which are connected to the three holes on the end bar.

9. Repeat steps 7 and 8 to connect the other six chains to the remaining end bar.

10. Make a new loop in the 24-gauge wire using the round-nose pliers. Slide the clasp onto this loop and hold the loop with the chain-nose pliers. Wrap the

wire around to secure and cut off the shorter wire end. Make a new loop on the leftover wire and slide it onto the outer loop of the end bar. Hold this wire loop with the chain-nose pliers and wrap the wire around the twist you just made. Cut off the excess wire.

11. On the other end bar, make a toggle by attaching a small bit of chain between ¼ and 1 inch (0.6 and 2.5 cm) in length. Do this by repeating step 10, substituting the toggle chain for the clasp. Be sure to use chain with large links for the toggle, so the clasp can attach to them.

12. Select one head pin and string one to three beads onto it. Bend the head pin 45°, and use the round-nose pliers to make a loop. Slide this loop onto the last link in the toggle chain. Hold the loop with the chain-nose pliers and wrap the wire around to secure. Cut off the excess wire.

13. Now it's time to bring life to the four-leaf clover in the middle of the bracelet. Select a head pin and slide on a few different stones, such as one 3-mm sterling silver bead, one 4-mm cherry quartz bead, and one 5-mm hematite rondelle. Bend the end of the head pin 45°, make a loop with the round-nose pliers, and slide it onto one of the leaves of the clover. Hold this loop with the chain-nose pliers and wrap the wire around to secure. Cut off the excess wire.

14. Repeat step 13 twenty-five times, varying the numbers and combinations of the stones. Place seven beaded head pins on the top and bottom leaves and six on the side leaves (three on either side of the chains).

Here's a handy little trick when attaching the head pins: Stick a piece of tape on the underside of the clover. This will help keep the head pins facing up so you can see which color stones you might want to add in any particular place as you're working. Remove the tape when you slide on another head pin, and press it back on when you want to see how the next group of stones will fall.

CHANDELIER

These earrings offer color and movement with their cascading tiers of beautiful garnet beads.

Finished size: 3½ inches (8.9 cm)

Materials

16 garnet beads, 7 mm

6 garnet beads, 4 mm

8-inch (20.3 cm) length of 1-mm
gold-filled chain

18-inch (45.7 cm) length of 22-gauge
gold-filled wire

32-inch (81.2 cm) length of 26-gauge
gold-filled wire

Tools

Round-nose pliers

Chain-nose pliers

Wire cutters

Large rubberized round-nose pliers

Ruler

Techniques

Making Twisted Wire Loop Links
(page 20)

Working with Head Pins (page 23)

Making Earring Loops (page 24)

Instructions

Make two

1. With wire cutters, cut off a 5-inch (12.7 cm) segment of the 22-gauge wire. Set aside this segment, as it will be used later to make the earring loops.

2. Cut the remaining 13 inches (33 cm) of 22-gauge wire in half, making two 6½-inch (16.5 cm) segments. These two pieces will be used to build the hangers from which all the stones dangle. (You could use a jig for making the wire base, but I prefer using round-nose pliers.)

3. Select one of the 6½-inch (16.5 cm) segments. Use the round-nose pliers to grip the middle of it. Wrap the wire one full turn to make a loop.

4. Hold this loop with the chain-nose pliers. Twist the wires around to secure.

5. Using the round-nose pliers again, place only the tip of one jaw in the center of the loop. Lightly grip the twist you just made and wrap the wires downward to make a second smaller loop. After the two wires have crossed, remove the round-nose pliers, hold onto this smaller loop with the chain-nose pliers, and twist again. The wires should now be horizontal with the loops on top (figure 1).

fig. 1

6. Place the round-nose pliers on one side of the loop in the wire, approximately ¼ inch (6 mm) away. Loop the wire around the jaw of the pliers.

7. Repeat this same action again ¼ inch (6 mm) away, this time wrapping the wire around a bit further down on the jaw of the pliers to make a larger loop. Continue wrapping the wire until you've wrapped around one and one-half times.

8. **fig. 2**

Repeat steps 6 and 7 on the other side of the loop (figure 2).

9. Using the rubberized round-nose pliers, slightly bend down the wire ends to give the hanger a pleasing curve. First, place the jaws of the pliers between the center loop and the smaller loop. Then nudge the end of the wire to shape it.

10. Repeat this between the smaller loop and the larger outer loop, nudging both sides to curve the hanger.

11. Repeat steps 9 and 10 on the other side to make both sides curve down slightly.

12. fig. 3

Now make the shortest dangle. Using the 26-gauge wire and the round-nose pliers, place the very end of the wire in the jaw tip of the pliers. Wrap the wire around the jaw two times.
After making the first loop, open up the jaws, turn the loop, clamp down again, and complete the second circle. While the pliers are still in place, bend the wire 45° to center the circled wire (figure 3).

13. Slide a 4-mm bead onto the wire and bend the wire 45°. Wrap it around using the round-nose pliers and slide it onto the end of the chain. Use the chain-nose pliers to hold onto this loop. Wrap the wire around to secure. For this design, I wrap the wire around the tops of the beads numerous times. If you would like to create this effect, continue wrapping the wire around and around until you are pleased with the look of it. Cut off the excess wire. You may also want to use the chain-nose pliers to gently press the tip of this wire inward, flush to the other wraps. This will prevent it from catching and possibly unraveling.

14. With the wire cutters, cut the attached chain ¼ inch (6 mm) from the bead.

15. Using the round-nose pliers, make a new loop with the 26-gauge wire. Slide the end of the chain onto the loop and wrap the loop closed. Slide on another 4-mm bead. Bend the wire 45° and make a new loop, this time a bit further along on the wire than usual. Slide the wire through the lower center loop on the wire hanger and pull it through.

16. Using the very tips of the chain-nose pliers, hold this loop beneath the wire hanger and wrap the wire around again to secure.

17. Now make the medium dangle. Start by making the end of this dangle. Repeat steps 12 and 13, this time using a 7-mm bead. Slide two ½-inch (1.3 cm) lengths of chain onto the top loop of the bead.

18. Attach a wire loop link with a 7-mm bead at the end of one piece of chain. Bend the wire and place it through one of the smaller loops on either side of the wire hanger. Wrap it closed to secure. Repeat with the remaining piece of chain, attaching it to the other smaller loop on the opposite side of the wire hanger.

19. Finally, make the longest dangle. Again starting from the end and working out, repeat steps 12 and 13, but use two beads, one 4-mm bead followed by one 7-mm bead. Attach two ¼-inch (6 mm) lengths of chain to this piece.

20. Make a wire loop link through one piece of chain and add another 7-mm bead. Before you close the loop, add a ⅜-inch (9.5 mm) segment of chain. Add a new wire loop link and 7-mm bead to the end of this piece of chain. Attach one last ¼-inch (6 mm) length of chain before you wrap the loop closed. Repeat this step on the remaining piece of chain you added in step 19.

21. Make a new loop in the 26-gauge wire and place one chain end onto the loop. Hold the loop with the chain-nose pliers and twist the wire around to secure. Cut off the shorter wire. Now loop the wire again and pass it through one of the end loops on the hanger. Hold the loop and wrap the wire around the twist. Cut off the excess.

22. Repeat step 21 with the remaining piece of chain.

23. Now make the earring loop. Take the 5-inch (12.7 cm) length of 22-gauge wire that you set aside in step 1. Cut it into two 2½-inch (6.4 cm) segments. Hold one of the wires with the round-nose pliers about ½ inch (1.3 cm) from the end. Loop the wire around. Slide the loop through the top loop of the hanger.

Hold the loop with the chain-nose pliers and twist the wires around to secure. Cut off the shorter wire.

24. Hold the wire with the rubberized round-nose pliers and loop the wire around to form the actual earring loop. Cut the wire to the desired length.

25. Now grip the very end of this same wire with the chain-nose pliers and bend it slightly upward to add a finishing detail (page 24).

SEA BUNDLE

Keep the essence of the sea close at hand when you wear a cluster of pearls, shells, tourmaline, and topaz.

Ring size: 5¼

Materials

2 copper-colored pearls (1 light, 1 dark), 6 mm

6 copper-colored pearls (3 light, 3 dark), 3 mm

2 dark green pearls, 5 mm

3 small shells in 3 different colors, 12 mm

1 dark blue tourmaline (indicolite) briolette, 5 mm

1 blue topaz briolette, 6 mm

1 light blue chalcedony briolette, 6 mm

10-inch (25.4 cm) length of 22-gauge gold-filled wire

18-inch (45.7 cm) length of 26-gauge gold-filled wire

Tools

Mandrel

Round-nose pliers

Wire cutters

Ruler

Glue

Techniques

Using Special Tools (mandrel and ring sizer, page 25)

Instructions

1. Determine the size for your ring (page 25). Begin working with the mandrel and the 22-gauge wire. Place the wire on the mandrel, about ¾ inch (1.9 cm) from the end. Wrap the wire around the mandrel three times.

2. Twist the ¾-inch (1.9 cm) end and the other end of the wire two times around to secure the wire in place. Cut the longer end to the same length as the shorter end.

3. Carefully remove the wire from the mandrel; it can easily unravel.

4. **fig. 1**

Wrap the 26-gauge wire around the bottom of the three 22-gauge wire loops to hold them together. First, twist the 26-gauge wire around two or three times, and then tuck in the shorter end so it is flush with the 22-gauge wire (figure 1).

5. **fig. 2**

Begin wrapping the longer wire around the bottom of the ring and over the end of the smaller 26-gauge wire (figure 2).

6. **fig. 3**

When you get to the tenth rotation, begin to wrap the wire less tightly, because you'll be sliding the wire back through the underside of these wires when you've finished wrapping. Continue wrapping five more times for a total of 15 rotations. Slide the end back through the underside of the wires to secure and conceal it. Pull the wire tight and cut off the excess (figure 3).

7. I recommend placing a drop of glue on both ends of the wire to secure it.

8. fig. 4

Returning to the top of the ring, use the round-nose pliers to twirl the two lengths of 22-gauge wire. Hold the very tip of one wire about one-third of the way up on the jaw of the pliers and start twisting the pliers around. You will have to let go and grab onto the wire as you go around. Twirl the wire all the way until you reach the ring (figure 4).

9. fig. 5

Wrap the remaining 26-gauge wire around one side of the top center point of the ring (adjacent to one of the spirals) and twist it together to secure (figure 5). Cut off the shorter wire.

10. Attach the stones and pearls. Begin by sliding on a pearl and secure it by wrapping the wire around the ring. Then, one by one, add more stones or pearls, each time wrapping the wire around the ring again. Continue to work, creating a free-flowing cluster. Move from one side of the twirled wire to the other and then back again. As you go along, try to fill in any spaces. Depending on the size of stones, pearls, and shells you are using, your finished product will (and should!) always look different each time you make this ring design. Let your imagination guide you.

11. After you've attached all of the stones, loop the 26-gauge wire you're working with around one side of the 22-gauge ring (under the stones). Wrap it around three to five times. Then repeat the looping and tucking process you did in step 6. Slide the wire back through, pull it tight, and cut off the excess wire.

OLÉ!

You'll be in the mood for a fiesta when you slip on these festive earrings, enhanced with silver wire loops styled on a jig.

Finished size: 3 inches (7.6 cm)

Materials

8 rose quartz briolettes (long), 6 mm

12 cherry quartz briolettes (round), 6 mm

8 clear quartz briolettes (round), 6 mm

2 sterling silver ball-post earrings with open rings

12-inch (30.5 cm) length of 5-mm sterling silver krinkle chain

26-inch (66 cm) length of 22-gauge sterling silver wire

28-inch (71.1 cm) length of 26-gauge sterling silver wire

Tools

Jig

Chain-nose pliers

Round-nose pliers

Wire cutters

Large rubberized round-nose pliers or flat nylon-jaw pliers

Ruler

Techniques

Making Twisted Wire Loop Links (page 20)

Working with Purchased Earring Findings (page 24)

Using Special Tools (jigs, page 25)

Designer's Tip

I used a jig with a curved grid to make these earrings. If you don't have one, you can adapt the pattern to a regular jig with straight holes, or you could even create the wire shape using round-nose pliers.

Instructions

Make two

1. The looped-wire framework for these earrings is made with a jig that has a curved grid.

2. **fig. 1**

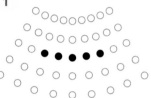

Place five pegs on the jig (figure 1). Using the 22-gauge wire, beginning about ½ inch (1.3 cm) from the end, wrap the wire around the

fig. 2

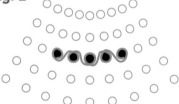

first peg, over and around the second peg, under and around the third peg, over and around the fourth peg, and under and around the fifth peg (figure 2). Make four of these five-hole shapes.

3. After carefully removing the wire shapes from the jig, use the rubberized round-nose pliers to flatten the middle holes. Don't flatten the outer holes.

4. **fig. 3**

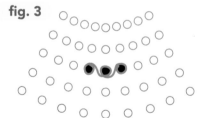

Make two additional shapes, this time using only three pegs instead of five. For these two shapes, wrap the wire over and around, under and around, and over and around (figure 3).

5. Cut the 12 inches (30.5 cm) of chain into twelve 1-inch (2.5 cm) segments. Count the links in the segments to make sure that all of them are exactly the same length.

6. Now the tricky part! Begin attaching these chain segments from the bottom of the earring, working toward the top, first looping the end links of the chain segments into the outer loops of one five-hole wire shape.

7. fig. 4

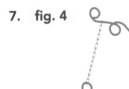

After the first two chains are attached to the bottom five-hole wire shape, attach these same chains onto the second five-hole wire shape. Ultimately, these chain ends should lie between the outer two loops on both sides of this second five-hole wire shape (figure 4). It's necessary to keep the chain as straight as possible as you attach it to the next wire shape. This may take a little bit of practice, as well as patience and repetition, to master the technique. Using the chain-nose pliers, close the two outer loops on the lower element.

8. fig. 5

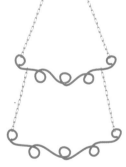

Follow this immediately by attaching two more chains to the outer loops of the second wire shape (figure 5). Then, pushing with the chain-nose pliers, close the two outer wire loops on the second wire shape.

9. fig. 6

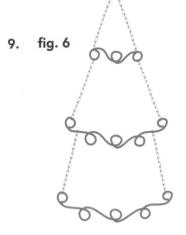

Set this piece aside and begin working on the earring from above. Attach two chain segments to one of the three-hole wire shapes. Then pick up the piece from step 8, which has two loose chains at the top, and slide those links onto these same two wire loops (figure 6). Use the chain-nose pliers to close the two outer wire loops on the top-most wire shape.

10. Finally, attach these two chain segments to the ring of the ball-post earring, using the chain-nose pliers to slightly bend the loop on the ring to one side. Place the two chain segments onto the loop and push the ring back into place. The framework of the earring is now complete.

11. To attach the briolettes, use the 26-gauge wire. Slide the wire through a 6-mm briolette, letting ¾ inch (1.9 cm) of the wire extend out the other side. Bend both wire ends up until they cross tightly. Twist the two wires together. Cut off the shorter wire end.

12. Bend the wire forward 45° and use the round-nose pliers to wrap it around into a loop. Slide the wire through one of the outer loops in the earring framework. Hold this wire loop with the chain-nose pliers and wrap the wire around the twist you made in step 11. Cut off the excess wire.

13. Continue to repeat steps 11 and 12, placing a total of 14 briolettes on the earring, with the four long briolettes in the center of the design. **Note:** When attaching the briolettes, all the loops in the briolettes should be side-facing to attach to the holes in the wire shapes, except for the top briolette, which attaches to the ring of the ball-post earring. This one needs a forward-facing loop (figure 7).

fig. 7
Forward facing
Side facing

CITY NIGHTS

Step out in style when you wear this exceptional necklace, a showpiece design made with jasper and garnets.

Finished size: Each strand, from shortest to longest: 18½ inches (47 cm); 23 inches (58.4 cm); 30 inches (76.2 cm)

Materials

10 ocean jasper beads, 14 mm

10 ocean jasper beads, 10 mm

5 ocean jasper beads, 8 mm

8 ocean jasper beads, 6 mm

10 honey jasper beads, 8 mm

18 garnet beads, 6 mm

10 rutile quartz beads, 4 mm

12 carnelian beads, 4 mm

1 gold-filled lobster clasp

75-inch (190.5 cm) length of 1.5-mm gold-filled chain

4-inch (10.2 cm) length of 22-gauge gold-filled wire

130-inch (330.2 cm) length of 24-gauge gold-filled wire

Tools

Chain-nose pliers

Round-nose pliers

Wire cutters

Large rubberized round-nose pliers

Ruler

Techniques

Making Twisted Wire Loop Links (page 20)

Making Catches and Clasps (page 22)

Instructions

fig. 1

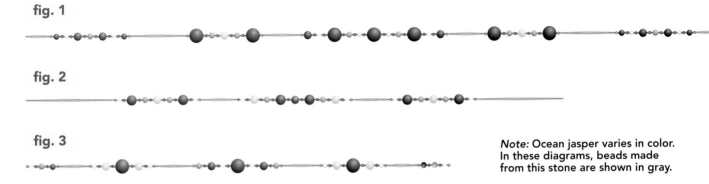

fig. 2

fig. 3

Note: Ocean jasper varies in color. In these diagrams, beads made from this stone are shown in gray.

1. Begin this necklace by making the longest strand, following the diagram in figure 1. Cut the chain to make 18 segments in the following lengths: six short segments each 1 inch (2.5 cm), six medium segments each 1½ inches (3.8 cm), and six long segments each 2¼ inches (5.7 cm). Count the links to make sure each segment is exactly the same length. You'll be adding the segments in groups of three. After the segments are attached at one end and you are ready to attach them at the other end, I recommend that you hang the strand so the chains will be dangling as you slide on the connecting wire loop. This helps ensure that the chain segments will be perfectly straight and not twisted or tangled as you attach them.

2. Make a loop in the 24-gauge wire about ¾ inch (1.9 cm) from the end using the round-nose pliers. Slide the end links of three 1-inch (2.5 cm) chain segments onto the wire loop. Hold the loop with the chain-nose pliers and twist the wire around to secure. Cut off the shorter wire end.

3. Slide on one 6-mm ocean jasper bead. Bend the wire 45° and loop it around using the round-nose pliers. Hold the loop with the chain-nose pliers and wrap the wire around to secure. Cut off the excess wire. Repeat the process of adding individual twisted wire bead links to the strand by making a new loop with the wire, sliding it into the loop you just completed, and placing the next bead. Follow this order: 4-mm rutile quartz bead, 8-mm jasper bead, 6-mm garnet bead, 8-mm jasper bead, 4-mm rutile quartz bead, 6-mm jasper bead. Before you close the loop for the last 6-mm jasper bead, slide on three 2¼-inch (5.7 cm) chain segments.

4. Make a new loop in the wire and slide the end links of the chain segments onto it. Add the next group of individual twisted wire bead links in this order: 14-mm jasper bead, 6-mm garnet bead, 8-mm honey jasper bead, 6-mm garnet bead, and 14-mm jasper bead. Before you close the loop for the last 14-mm jasper bead, slide on three 1½-inch (3.8 cm) chain segments.

5. Make a new loop in the wire and slide the end links of the chain segments onto it. Add the next group of individual twisted wire bead links in this order: 8-mm jasper bead, 4-mm carnelian bead, 14-mm jasper bead, 6-mm garnet bead, 4-mm rutile quartz bead, 14-mm jasper bead, 4-mm rutile quartz bead, 6-mm garnet bead, 14-mm jasper bead, 4-mm carnelian bead, and 8-mm jasper bead. Before you close the loop for the last 8-mm jasper bead, slide on three 1½-inch (3.8 cm) chain segments. The 14-mm jasper bead in the middle of this segment is the center of this strand.

6. To complete this strand, you'll add the same group of individual twisted wire bead links that you added in step 4, but this time you'll slide on three 2¼-inch (5.7 cm) chain segments. Then, you'll finish

by adding the same group of individual twisted wire bead links that you added in step 3, sliding on the remaining three 1-inch (2.5 cm) chain segments. You should now have a perfectly symmetrical strand.

Now that you've finished the long strand, set it aside and make the medium and short ones. After all three are finished, you will attach them together.

7. For the medium strand, follow figure 2. Cut the chain to make 12 segments in the following lengths: six short segments each 1½ inches (3.8 cm) and six long segments each 3½ inches (8.9 cm). Follow the directions in step 1 for counting the links and attaching the chain segments.

8. Make a loop in the 24-gauge wire about ¾ inch (1.9 cm) from the end using the round-nose pliers. Slide the end links of three 3½-inch (8.9 cm) chain segments onto the wire loop. Hold the loop with the chain-nose pliers and twist the wire around to secure. Cut off the shorter wire end.

9. Slide on one 4-mm carnelian bead. Bend the wire 45° and loop it around using the round-nose pliers. Hold the loop with the chain-nose pliers and wrap the wire around to secure. Cut off the excess wire. Repeat the process of adding individual twisted wire bead links to the strand by making a new loop with the wire, sliding it into the loop you just completed, and placing the next bead. Follow this order: 10-mm ocean jasper bead, 6-mm garnet bead, 8-mm honey jasper bead, 6-mm garnet bead, 10-mm ocean jasper bead, and 4-mm carnelian bead. Before you close the loop for the last 4-mm carnelian bead, slide on three 1½-inch (3.8 cm) chain segments.

10. Make a new loop in the wire and slide the end links of the chain segments onto it. Add the next group of individual twisted wire bead links in this order: 4-mm carnelian bead, 8-mm honey jasper bead, 6-mm garnet bead, 10-mm ocean jasper bead, 8-mm ocean jasper bead, 10-mm ocean jasper bead, 6-mm garnet

bead, 8-mm honey jasper bead, and 4-mm carnelian bead. Before you close the loop for the last 4-mm carnelian bead, slide on the three remaining 1½-inch (3.8 cm) chain segments. The 8-mm ocean jasper bead in the middle of this segment is the center of this strand.

11. To complete this strand, you'll add the same group of individual twisted wire bead links that you added in step 9, but this time you'll slide on the remaining three 3½-inch (8.9 cm) chain segments.

Now that you've finished the medium strand, set it aside and make the short one.

12. To make the short strand, see figure 3. Cut the chain to make six segments in the following lengths: six segments each 1¼ inches (3.2 cm) and six segments each 1½ inches (3.8 cm). Follow the directions in step 1 for counting the links and attaching the chain segments.

13. Make a loop in the 24-gauge wire and place three of the 1¼ inches (3.2 cm) pieces of chain on the loop. Hold the loop with the chain-nose pliers and twist the wires together. Cut off the shorter wire end.

14. Slide one 6-mm jasper bead onto the wire. Bend the wire 45° and loop it around using the round-nose pliers. Hold the loop with the chain-nose pliers and wrap the loop around to secure. Cut off the excess wire.

15. Repeat the process of adding individual twisted wire bead links to the strand by making a new loop with the wire, sliding it into the loop you just completed, and placing the next bead. Add one 6-mm garnet bead and then one 4-mm carnelian bead in this fashion. After you add the carnelian bead, hold the wire loop and wrap it around to secure. Cut off the excess wire.

16. Add twisted wire bead links to the opposite end of the group of chains. Follow this bead order: 4-mm rutile quartz bead, 8-mm honey jasper bead, 14-mm jasper bead, 8-mm honey jasper bead, and 4-mm

rutile quartz bead. Before you close the loop for the last 4-mm quartz bead, slide on three 1½-inch (3.8 cm) chain segments.

17. Repeat the process of adding individual twisted wire bead links to the strand by making a new loop with the wire, sliding it into the end links of the chain segments, and placing the next bead. Add the next group of individual beads in this order: 6-mm garnet bead, 8-mm jasper bead, 4-mm carnelian bead, 14-mm jasper bead, 4-mm carnelian bead, 8-mm jasper bead, and a 6-mm garnet bead. Before you close the loop for the last 6-mm garnet bead, slide on the three remaining 1½-inch (3.8 cm) chain segments. The 14-mm ocean jasper bead in the middle of this segment is the center of this strand.

18. To complete this strand, you'll add the same group of individual twisted wire bead links that you added in step 16, but you'll slide on the remaining three 1¼-inch (3.2 cm) chain segments. Then, you'll finish by adding the same group of individual twisted wire bead links that you added in steps 14 and 15. After adding the final 4-mm carnelian bead, wrap the loop to secure and cut away the excess wire.

19. Make a loop in the 22-gauge wire about ¾ inch (1.9 cm) from the end using the round-nose pliers. Slide this loop through the lobster clasp. Hold the loop with the chain-nose pliers and twist the wires around to secure. Cut off the shorter wire. Slide one 6-mm jasper bead onto the wire and bend the wire 45°. Loop the wire around using the round-nose pliers.

20. fig. 4

Slide all three strands onto this loop in the following order: first, the three chains of the long strand; second, the three chains of the medium strand; and third, the loop at the end of the short strand. Hold the loop containing all your strands with the chain-nose pliers and wrap the wire around to secure. Continue wrapping the wire around several times to add extra looping detail (figure 4). After wrapping the wire around about five times, cut off the excess.

21. Using the 22-gauge wire and the rubberized round-nose pliers, make a large loop about ¾ inch (1.9 cm) from the end. Hold this large loop with these pliers and twist the wires around. Cut off the shorter wire end. String on one 6-mm jasper bead and bend the wire 45°. Loop the wire around using the round-nose pliers.

22. This time, slide the other end of all three strands onto this loop, again using the same order: first, the three chains of the long strand; second, the three chains of the medium necklace; and third, the loop at the end of the short strand. Hold this new loop with the chain-nose pliers and wrap the wire around. Continue wrapping the wire around several times to add extra looping detail. After wrapping the wire around about five times, cut off the excess.

SUNSET

Shell pearls in vivid peaches and pinks combine to create an artistic display in this eye-catching, multi-strand bracelet.

Instructions

Finished size: 7⅝ inches (19.4 cm)

Materials

3 shell pearls in bright pink, 16 mm

4 shell pearls in peach, 14 mm

4 shell pearls in medium pink, 12 mm

18 shell pearls in light pink, 8 mm

20 shell pearls in lightest pink, 4 mm

24 smoky quartz beads, 4 mm

20 gold-filled beads, 2 mm

4 gold-filled beads, 3 mm

1 gold-filled four-strand slide clasp

6-inch length of 1.5-mm
    gold-filled chain

38-inch length of 24-gauge
    gold-filled wire

Tools

Chain-nose pliers

Round-nose pliers

Wire cutters

Ruler

Techniques

Making Twisted Wire Loop Links
    (page 20)

1. To make this bracelet, start from the outside and work your way in. Separate the two slide clasp pieces while making the bracelet, always being careful to attach each strand to the correct loop. Using the round-nose pliers and the 24-gauge wire, create a loop about ¾ inch (1.9 cm) from the end of the wire. Slide the loop through one of the outer loops on one of the pieces of the slide clasp. Hold the wire loop with the chain-nose pliers and twist the wire around. Cut off the shorter wire end.

2. Slide on the following beads: one 4-mm smoky quartz bead, one 2-mm gold-filled bead, one 4-mm shell pearl bead, one 2-mm gold-filled bead, and one 12-mm shell pearl bead.

3. Bend the wire about 45° and, using the round-nose pliers, make a loop in the wire. Slide the chain onto the loop. Hold the loop with the chain-nose pliers and wrap the wire around to secure. Cut off the excess wire.

4. Cut off all the chain, leaving only one link attached. (If you prefer, you can use a jump ring here instead of one link of the chain.) Using your fingers, curve this just-finished beaded wire to form a slight outward-facing curve (figure 1).

fig. 1

5. Using the round-nose pliers, make a new loop in the wire approximately ¾ inch (1.9 cm) from the end. Slide the wire through the one link of chain you attached in step 4. Hold the loop with the chain-nose pliers and wrap the wire around. Cut off the shorter wire end.

6. Slide on the following beads: one 4-mm smoky quartz bead, one 2-mm gold-filled bead, one 4-mm shell pearl bead, one 3-mm gold-filled bead, one 4-mm shell pearl bead, one 2-mm gold-filled bead, and one 4-mm smoky quartz bead.

7. **fig. 2**   Repeat steps 3 and 4 of looping the wire, attaching it to
    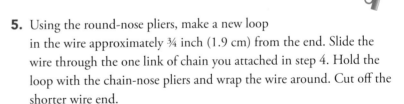   one chain link (or use a jump ring, if you prefer), and curving the beaded wire (figure 2).

8. Make a loop in the wire using the round-nose pliers. Slide it through the one link of chain. Holding the loop with the chain-nose pliers, wrap the wire around to secure it. Cut off the shorter wire end.

9. Slide one 4-mm smoky quartz bead, one 14-mm shell pearl bead, and one smoky quartz bead onto the wire.

10. Repeat steps 3 and 4 of looping the wire, attaching it to chain or a jump ring, and curving the beaded wire.

11. Loop the wire again using the round-nose pliers, slide it through the link of chain, and wrap the wire around with the chain-nose pliers. Cut off the shorter wire end.

12. Slide on the following beads: one 4-mm shell pearl bead, one 2-mm gold-filled bead, one 4-mm smoky quartz bead, one 8-mm shell pearl bead, one 4-mm smoky quartz bead, one 2-mm gold-filled bead, and one 4-mm shell pearl bead.

13. Repeat steps 3 and 4 of looping the wire, attaching it to chain or a jump ring, and curving the beaded wire.

14. You've now arrived just past the midpoint of the first strand. Make three more curved beaded sections before attaching this strand to the opposite end of the slide clasp. For these beaded sections, repeat the bead sequence used in steps 9, 6, and 2, in that order, but attach the section from step 2 in reverse order, so it mirrors the other end of the strand.

15. fig. 3

After making the final curve, attach the strand to the slide clasp; make sure the pieces of the clasp are oriented as shown when you attach the strand (figure 3).

16. fig. 4

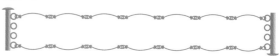

You've now finished the first strand. Repeat this entire strand, working steps 1 through 15, for the other outer loops of the slide clasp (figure 4). Be especially careful to attach each strand to the correct loop of the clasp.

17. Now make the inner strands of the bracelet. Make a loop with 24-gauge wire using the round-nose pliers. Slide this loop through one of the inner loops on one of the pieces of the slide clasp.

18. Hold the wire loop with the chain-nose pliers and twist the wire around. Cut off the shorter wire end.

19. Make a new loop in the wire using round-nose pliers. Holding this second loop with the chain-nose pliers, wrap the wire around the twist you made in step 18. Cut off the excess wire.

20. Make a new loop in the wire ¾ inch (1.9 cm) from the end. Slide this loop through the twisted wire loop attached to the slide clasp. Using the chain-nose pliers, hold this loop and twist the wires around. Cut off the shorter wire end.

21. fig. 5

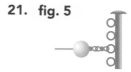

Slide on one 8-mm shell pearl bead (figure 5-930) and make a new loop in the wire. Place ⅜ inch (9.5 mm) of chain on the loop, hold that loop with the chain-nose pliers, and wrap the wire around to secure the chain.

22. Repeat steps 17 through 21 for the other inner loop on the slide clasp.

23. Create a new loop with the wire and place both chain ends on this loop. Hold the loop with the chain-nose pliers and wrap the wire around to secure. Cut off the shorter wire end.

24. Slide one 16-mm shell pearl bead onto the wire. Loop the wire again, attaching two more ⅜-inch (9.5 mm) chain lengths to this loop before you secure it.

25. Make a new loop with the wire and attach it to one of the pieces of chain you added in step 24. Twist the wire around to secure the loop and cut off the shorter wire end. Slide on one 8-mm shell pearl bead and loop the wire again. Attach another ⅜-inch (9.5 mm) length of chain. Wrap the wire around to secure the loop and cut off the excess wire. Repeat this step with the other piece of chain.

26. Repeat steps 24 and 25 two more times to arrive at the other end of the bracelet.

27. fig. 6

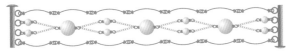

Make twisted wire loop links to attach each strand to the slide clasp (figure 6).

28. Next, attach the central strand of the bracelet to the outer strands. Make a loop with the 24-gauge wire. Slide this loop through one of the loops at either side of the 16-mm shell pearl bead in the center. Using the chain-nose pliers, hold the loop and wrap the wires around. Cut off the shorter wire end.

29. fig. 7

Slide one 8-mm shell pearl bead onto the wire and loop the wire again. Make this loop perpendicular to the first loop, instead of both facing the same way. (When completed, the loop should appear as in figure 7.)

30. fig. 8

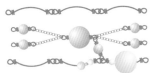

Slide this loop through the two loops from the outer strands that are joined by the single link of chain. The little chain link that was there to hold it all together will now be encircled by this new wire loop. Wrap the wire to secure the loop and cut off the excess wire (figure 8).

31. Repeat steps 28 through 30 three more times until all sides of the center bead are attached.

32. fig. 9

Using one 4-mm shell pearl bead and one 8-mm shell pearl bead, make the same connections as in steps 28 through 30, placing these sections on the inner side of the two remaining 16-mm beads (figure 9).

The Brown and Sharp (B&S) Gauge for Sheet Metal

Gauge Number	Thickness in inches	Thickness in millimeters
0	0.3249	8.2525
1	0.2893	7.3482
2	0.2576	6.5430
3	0.2294	5.8268
4	0.2043	5.1892
5	0.1819	4.6203
6	0.1620	4.1148
7	0.1443	3.6652
8	0.1285	3.2639
9	0.1144	2.9058
10	0.1019	2.5883
11	0.0907	2.3038
12	0.0808	2.0523
13	0.0720	1.8288
14	0.0641	1.6281
15	0.0571	1.4503
16	0.0508	1.2903
17	0.0453	1.1506
18	0.0403	1.0236
19	0.0359	0.9119
20	0.0320	0.8128
21	0.0285	0.7239
22	0.0253	0.6426
23	0.0226	0.5740
24	0.0201	0.5105
25	0.0179	0.4547
26	0.0159	0.4039
27	0.0142	0.3607
28	0.0126	0.3200
29	0.0113	0.2870
30	0.0100	0.2540

Standard Stone and Bead Sizes

To help you in planning your jewelry, here is a chart that illustrates the size of gemstone beads. All the sizes are shown in millimeters.

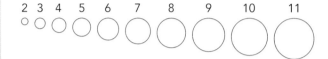

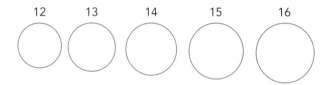

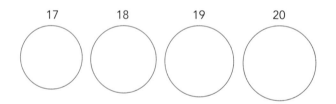

Appendix: Identifying Gemstones

Here is a list that briefly describes each of the types of gemstones used for the pieces in this book. Many consider gemstones to have healing qualities, so I've included that, too. It's all a part of what makes gemstones so alluring to those who love to make, wear, and share their jewelry.

Agate

Color: All colors

Several well-known types of agate include fire agate, moss agate, eye agate, and tree agate. It's famous for its colorful banding, which is caused by the presence of various impurities. It is often found in geode form with crystals of quartz. Agate is a type of chalcedony.

Hardness: 7

Healing values: Agate is considered to have grounding and calming qualities, balancing yin and yang as well as the physical and the emotional.

Amber

Color: Mostly golden yellow and brown but can also be green, red, violet, and black

Amber is an organic mineral created when pine-tree resin fossilized 50 million years ago. It may contain insects, moss, pine needles, and sometimes larger things, such as frogs, toads, and lizards that were trapped in the resin when it was still sticky. Amber is very light; it can float in water. When burned, it gives off the smell of incense. Be careful of imitations, because plastic or glass is often used to replicate amber.

Hardness: 2.5

Healing values: Amber is believed to release stress, clear the body of disease, and dissolve negative energy, bringing about patience, wisdom, and balance.

Amethyst

Colors: Purple, lilac, and mauve

Amethyst is a crystalline variety of quartz found inside geodes of volcanic rock. The purple color is caused by trace amounts of ferric iron.

Hardness: 7

Healing values: Amethyst is considered to be the stone of spirituality and contentment, opening up the throat chakra and channels to one's higher self, with calming qualities for meditation.

Apatite

Colors: Colorless, pink, yellow, green, blue, violet, and brown

The colors of apatite vary extensively, but they are usually very bright and strong. They can also be transparent or opaque. The name comes from the Greek word for *cheat*, because apatite has often been confused with other stones. It is a common stone, appearing in many different types of rock.

Hardness: 5

Healing values: Apatite is believed to be a healing stone, helping with communication and teaching, balancing energy, stimulating intellect, and dissolving negativity.

Aventurine

Colors: Green, reddish brown, and golden brown

The color found in this quartz variety is caused by inclusions of green fuchsite mica, pyrite, goethite, or hematite. Aventurine has often been confused with aventurine feldspar, amazonite, and jade.

Hardness: 7

Healing values: Aventurine is believed to assist with balancing the male-female energies, boosting creativity, and providing joy and clarity.

Carnelian

Colors: Shades of red, orange, and brown

Carnelian is part of the chalcedony variety of quartz. The color, which can be translucent or opaque, is due to trace values of iron oxide.

Hardness: 7

Healing values: Carnelian is believed to help ground oneself in the present, bring about good choices in business, and aid fertility.

Chalcedony

Colors: Bluish gray to whitish gray

Chalcedony is the name for all of the microcrystalline quartzes, such as agate, chrysoprase, jasper, and carnelian, but it is also used specifically to refer to the bluish white, gray variety. It is a very porous stone, a quality that makes it suitable for dyes.

Hardness: 7

Healing values: Chalcedony is believed to remove hostility and bring about benevolence and the maternal instinct.

Chrysoprase

Color: Apple green

Chrysoprase, its color due to the presence of nickel, is considered the most valuable kind of chalcedony.

Hardness: 7

Healing values: This stone is thought to relax the body and mind, energize the heart chakra, remove ego, and help with creativity and talent.

Citrine

Colors: Light yellow, dark yellow, and golden brown

Citrine, aptly named after the word citrus, is the yellow variety of crystal quartz. Its color is due to the presence of iron.

Hardness: 7

Healing values: Citrine is considered to be the stone of prosperity, bringing happiness, energy, and creativity.

Coral

Colors: Red, pink, orange, white, black, blue, and gold

Coral is the secreted skeleton from the marine organism called coral polyps. In its natural state, coral is dull, but it has a glassy luster when polished.

Hardness: 3

Healing values: Coral symbolizes life and energy, and it is often used as an aid in meditation and visualization.

Fluorite

Colors: Colorless as well as a wide range of colors, including yellow, blue, pink, purple, and green

Fluorite often forms in a cubic formation and can be fluorescent under ultraviolet light. Its name is derived from the Latin word for flow.

Hardness: 4

Healing values: Fluorite is believed to help bring order to chaos, as well as protect and sustain health, intellect, and emotional well-being.

Garnet

Colors: Various forms of garnet range from colorless, green, and yellow to shades of red and orange.

The rich red color associated with garnet is due to the presence of iron and chromium. The name *garnet* comes from the Latin word for pomegranate.

Hardness: 6.5 to 7.5

Healing values: The varieties of garnet are believed to have a number of healing qualities, including bringing about creativity and fostering love.

Hematite

Color: Blackish gray, brownish red, and metallic

Hematite's metallic luster can give it the appearance of metal. It has been called bloodstone because the saw coolant becomes blood-red during the cutting process. Hematite is also used to make red ocher for painting. It is found in fossils, where it filled in the spaces as the organic material disintegrated.

Hardness: 5.5 to 6.5

Healing values: Hematite is considered to have grounding and balancing qualities, aiding concentration and removing negativity.

Jade

Colors: Usually green, but also all colors

The two varieties of jade (jadeite and nephrite) are so similar that they were thought to be variations of the same stone until 1863, when they were defined as two different varieties. Jade is a very tough stone, making it excellent for carving.

Hardness: 6 to 7

Healing values: A symbol of serenity and purity, jade is believed to bring harmony to relationships, calming the emotions while bringing passion.

Jasper

Colors: Shades of brown, gray, blue, red, yellow, orange, and green

Jasper is part of the chalcedony family of quartz. It is opaque and comes in a variety of looks; orbicular and ocean jasper have white or gray eye-shaped patterns surrounded with red, while the ribbon or riband variety is striped.

Hardness: 7

Healing values: Jasper is believed to be the supreme nurturer, helping with grounding and organization, and it is the patron stone of counselors and healers.

Kyanite

Colors: Shades of blue, white, gray, and green

Kyanite is easily identified by its streaks. It can be transparent or translucent and has a glassy or pearly luster.

Hardness: 5 to 7

Healing values: Kyanite is believed to align all the chakras, bringing tranquility and calming; it does not accumulate or retain negative energy.

Labradorite

Colors: Dark gray or black, with multicolored iridescence

Labradorite is named after Labrador, the Canadian peninsula where it was discovered. It is part of the feldspar (rock) group. Due to its unique iridescence resembling an oil slick, also known as labradorescence, it is often fashioned as a gem.

Hardness: 6

Healing values: Labradorite is considered a protective stone, deflecting unwanted energies and relieving stress.

Lapis lazuli

Colors: Blue, greenish blue, and violet

Lapis lazuli is a rock, while most other gemstones are minerals. The color agent is sulfur, and it is usually found with white marble.

Hardness: 5.5

Healing values: Known as a stone of protection and enlightenment, lapis lazuli is believed to release stress, focus thoughts, and promote creativity.

Malachite

Colors: Banded, light and dark green

The green color of malachite is caused by the presence of copper. Malachite, which is often attached to copper in its natural state, grows in shell-like formations, creating rings, lines, and other shapes.

Hardness: 4

Healing values: Often considered to be the stone of transformation, malachite is thought to clear a path for desired goals, bringing fidelity in love and clarifying emotions.

Moonstone

Colors: White, light yellow, and light blue

Moonstone is a rock (not a mineral), a member of the feldspar group. As with labradorite, moonstone is fashioned for jewelry because of its beauty. It has an opalescence, similar to a soap bubble, which is caused by light reflecting off its internal structure.

Hardness: 6

Healing values: Moonstone is considered to be the stone of feminine intuition, also helping to find fulfillment of one's destiny.

Onyx

Colors: Usually black with white bands

Onyx is part of the chalcedony family of minerals. The sardonyx variety has brownish red bands; marble onyx, not a true onyx, contains colors including yellow and green. Onyx is similar to agate, with the difference that onyx bands are straight, and agate bands are curved. These straight bands have made onyx a favorite stone for carving cameos.

Hardness: 7

Healing values: Onyx is considered to be a stone of strength, bringing about stamina as well as self-confidence, and helping to focus the mind and absorb sorrow.

Pearl

Colors: White, silver, cream, golden, pink, green, blue, and black

Pearls are formed inside mollusks as a defense against irritants such as sand. The color of a natural pearl depends on the type of mollusk that formed it. Because of the porous quality of pearls, they are often found in a variety of other colors artificially created through the use of dyes. Cultured pearls are formed when humans replicate this natural process, creating pearls that are available in interesting variations of color and shape, even though they lack the innate beauty of natural pearls. The quality of cultured pearls varies, but they are much less expensive than natural pearls. I've used a lot of disk-shaped cultured pearls for pieces in this book. Shell pearls are manufactured from the seashells, then coated and polished to produce pearl-like beads. Because shell pearls are man-made, you'll find a wide range of quality, shape, size, and color.

Hardness: 3

Healing values: Pearls symbolize purity, spiritual transformation, charity, honesty, wisdom, and all the best within us. They are believed to reduce oversensitivity, bringing about peacefulness.

Peridot

Colors: Green and olive green

Peridot is the name given to the gem-quality version of the olivine mineral. Its green color is caused by the presence of iron.

Hardness: 6.5

Healing values: Peridot is considered to be a cleansing stone, bringing about clarity and well-being, aiding in understanding the purpose of life, and opening and clarifying the heart and solar plexus chakras.

Quartz

Colors: Various (see five common varieties below)

Quartz is the name for not only the clear crystal variety of this mineral, but also many colored crystal varieties, as well as the massive microcrystalline varieties such as chalcedony, agate, and carnelian. Amethyst, citrine, and other gemstones are also in the quartz family, but you'll find them listed separately here because they are more commonly known by their unique names.

Hardness: 7

Clear quartz

Color: Colorless

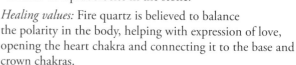

Clear quartz, also known as rock crystal, is one of the most common minerals on the Earth's crust.

Healing values: This is believed to be one of the most powerful stones for healing, and it is used widely for meditation and cleansing the soul.

Fire (harlequin) quartz

Colors: Colorless with red inclusions

The redness of fire quartz, also known as harlequin quartz, is caused by filaments of hematite or lepidocrocite in the stone.

Healing values: Fire quartz is believed to balance the polarity in the body, helping with expression of love, opening the heart chakra and connecting it to the base and crown chakras.

Rose quartz

Colors: Bright to pale pink

The pink color in rose quartz is caused by the presence of manganese or titanium. The stone is almost always cloudy and very brittle.

Healing values: Rose quartz is considered to be the stone of love, opening the heart chakra by releasing blocked emotions, with the further benefit of aiding fertility.

Rutile quartz

Color: Clear with needle-like crystal inclusions, which can be red, black, and gold

The hair or needle-like inclusions in rutile quartz are caused by strands of the mineral rutile. Tourmaline can cause a similar effect as rutile and is called tourmalinated quartz.

Healing values: Rutile quartz is believed to help in solving problems and to increase sexual desire.

Smoky quartz

Color: Smoky brown to black

Sometimes smoky quartz appears clear when first excavated, but it changes to a smoky color when exposed to the air.

Healing values: Smoky quartz is believed to aid in detoxification, cleansing and grounding the base chakra, while its calming qualities replace depression and fear with calm and positive thoughts.

Shells (including abalone)

Colors: Pink, peach, white, and black; abalone: iridescent blue-green

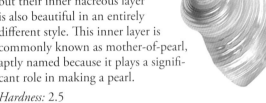

Shells are not only lovely in shape, but their inner nacreous layer is also beautiful in an entirely different style. This inner layer is commonly known as mother-of-pearl, aptly named because it plays a significant role in making a pearl.

Hardness: 2.5

Healing values: Shells represent the tides of emotion, bringing about the easy flow of feelings and sensitivities to others.

Topaz

Colors: Colorless, yellow, orange, pink, red, brown, green, blue, and violet

The name of this stone is derived from the island in the Red Sea originally named Topazius, now known as Zabargad.

Hardness: 8

Healing values: Topaz is believed to sooth, heal, and stimulate, opening the throat chakra and helping with verbalization.

Tourmaline

Colors: Varieties include colorless, pink/red, blue, yellow/brown, green/pink, green, and black

Tourmaline has a complex chemistry, which not only brings about its variety of colors but also other fascinating qualities. For example, when a tourmaline crystal is warmed, one end becomes positively charged and the other negatively charged, attracting dust!

Hardness: 7.5

Healing values: Tourmaline is considered a super activator of the heart chakra, converting dense energy into lighter energy, releasing tension, balancing the right and left brain, and bringing about inspiration and prosperity.

Turquoise

Colors: Light blue, blue-green, and green

The color of turquoise, whether primarily blue or green, is determined by the amount of iron or copper in it. The name comes from "Turkish stone," because the early trade routes bringing the stones to Europe from the Middle East and China passed through Turkey.

Hardness: 6

Healing values: Turquoise is believed to be a healing and purifying stone, helping with spiritual alignment and creativity.

Acknowledgments

I am endlessly grateful for the opportunity to share my passion for creating jewelry through this book. There's no doubt that I could not have done it without the love and support of my family, friends, and colleagues.

Mom, Dad, Nathalie, and Sylvie—thank you for believing in me from the very beginning, and supporting me as my jewelry grew from a hobby to another career. You've always been my rock and given me the best publicity!

Ron—Thank you for putting this opportunity together. I'm forever grateful.

Bryan—Your patience, support, and understanding was and is invaluable. Thank you for putting up with me and my rocks, as well as being my best judge of what works and what doesn't work as each piece came to fruition.

Valerie Shrader, Vivian Rothe, and Nathalie Mornu—I wish every first-time author could be lucky enough to work with such a supportive and encouraging editorial team. I'm so glad we were able to go on this journey together! Thanks also to art director Kristi Pfeffer for lending all her creativity to the book's layout.

Chevron Trading Post & Bead Company—This shop (based in Asheville, N.C.) generously loaned many of the beads pictured in the Basics section.

I also want to say a very special thank-you to all the brides and opera singers for whom I have been fortunate enough to create original, one-of-a-kind jewelry to be worn at some of their most important events. I've been honored.

Last, but not least, I want to thank all of my many friends and family around the world who have gotten the word out about my work by wearing my jewelry, and have also been by my side each step of the way.

Index